<u>Introduction to Our NEAB Rev</u>

Coordination Group Publications was set up with the aim of produ material for the National Curriculum. Following popular demand w... .aken our very successful Revision Guides for GCSE double science and from them produced a number of syllabus-specific versions for the NEAB and SEG double science syllabuses.

These brilliant NEAB Modular Science Revision Guides have <u>Three Top Features</u>:

Careful and Complete Explanations

Unlike other revision guides, we do not restrict ourselves to a brief outline of the bare essentials. Instead we work hard to give complete, concise and carefully written details on each topic.

Deliberate Use of Humour

We consider the humour to be an essential part of our Revision Guides. It is there to keep the reader interested and entertained, and we are certain that it greatly assists their learning. (It is not however expected to win us any awards...)

Carefully Matched to the NEAB Modular Syllabus, and more...

We have taken great care to ensure that this book follows the exact detail of the NEAB modular syllabus. Once again however we feel that merely illustrating the syllabus is an inadequate approach. We have therefore done rather more than simply list the basic syllabus details and add pictures. Instead we have endeavoured to include all the relevant explanation which appears to us to be necessary.   The result is a full 108 pages giving a clear explanation of the whole syllabus content. We hope you will appreciate the amount of time and care which has gone into this.

The early modules include material needed in the final exam. This material is contained in blue boxes (like this one) throughout the Early Modules Revision Guide.

Buy our books — they're ace

Final Exam

Contents

Final Exam   Contents

Module Eleven   Forces

Module Twelve   Waves and Radiation

(NEAB Syllabus reference)

Published by Coordination Group Publications Ltd.
Typesetting and Layout by The Coordination Group
Illustrations by: Sandy Gardner, e-mail: illustations@sandygardner.co.uk
and Bowser, Colorado USA

Coordinated by:
Paul Burton BSc (Hons)

Design Editors:
Chris Dennett BSc (Hons)
Theo Haywood BSc (Hons)

ISBN 1 84146 906 8

Groovy website: www.cgpbooks.co.uk

Printed by Elanders Hindson, Newcastle upon Tyne.
Clipart sources: CorelDRAW and VECTOR.
1199

Population Size & Distribution

Four Factors affect the Individual Organisms

These four physical factors fluctuate throughout the day and year. Organisms _live, grow_ and _reproduce_ in places where, and at times when, these conditions are suitable.

1) The _TEMPERATURE_ — this is rarely ideal for any organism.

2) The availability of _WATER_ — vital to all living organisms.

3) The _AMOUNT OF LIGHT AVAILABLE_ — this is most important to plants, but it also affects the visibility for animals.

4) _OXYGEN_ and _CARBON DIOXIDE_ — these affect respiration and photosynthesis respectively.

The Size of any Population depends on Five Factors

1) The _TOTAL AMOUNT OF FOOD_ or nutrients available.
2) The amount of _COMPETITION_ there is (from other species) for the same food or nutrients.
3) The _AMOUNT OF LIGHT AVAILABLE_ (this applies only to plants really).
4) The _NUMBER OF PREDATORS_ (or grazers) who may eat the animal (or plant) in question.
5) _DISEASE_.

All these factors help to explain why the _types_ of organisms vary from _place to place_ and from _time to time_.

The dynamics of plant and animal populations are really quite similar:
Plants often compete with each other for _space_, and for _water_ and _nutrients_ from the soil.
Animals often compete with each other for _space_, _food_ and _water_.

Generally organisms will thrive best if:

1) _THERE'S PLENTY OF THE GOOD THINGS IN LIFE_: food, water, space, shelter, light, etc.

2) _THEY'RE BETTER THAN THE COMPETITION AT GETTING IT_ (better _adapted_).

3) _THEY DON'T GET EATEN_.

4) _THEY DON'T GET ILL_.

That's pretty much the long and the short of it, wouldn't you say? So learn those four things. Every species is different, of course, but those _FOUR_ basic principles will always apply.

In Exam questions _YOU_ have to apply them to any new situation to work out what'll happen.

Revision stress — don't let it eat you up...

It's a strange topic is population sizes. In a way it seems like common sense, but it all seems to get so messy. Anyway, _learn all the points on this page_ and you'll be OK with it, I'd think.

Adapt and Survive

If you *learn the features* that make these animals and plants well adapted, you'll be able to apply them to any other similar creatures they might give you in the Exam.
Chances are you'll get a *camel*, *cactus* or *polar bear* anyway.

The Polar Bear — Designed for Arctic Conditions

The *Polar bear* has all these features: (which *many other arctic creatures* have too, so think on...)

1) *Large size* and *compact shape* (i.e. rounded), including dinky little ears, to keep the *surface area* to a *minimum* (compared to the body weight) — this all *reduces heat loss*.
2) A thick layer of *blubber* for *insulation* and food storage.
3) *Thick hairy coat* for keeping the body heat in.
4) *Greasy fur* which *sheds water* after swimming to *prevent cooling* due to evaporation.
5) *White fur* to match the surroundings for *camouflage*.
6) *Strong swimmer* and *runner* to catch food in the water and on land.
7) *Big feet* to *spread the weight* on snow and ice.

The Camel — Designed for Desert Conditions

The *camel* has all these features: (most of which are shared by *other desert creatures*...)

1) All *fat* is stored in the *hump*, there is *no layer of body fat*. This helps it to *lose* body heat.
2) *Large surface area*. The shape of a camel is anything but compact, which gives it more surface area to *lose body heat* to its surroundings.
3) It can *store* a lot of *water* without problem. Up to *20 gallons* at once.
4) Its *sandy colour* gives good *camouflage*.
5) *Large feet* to *spread load* on soft sand.
6) It *loses very little water*. There's little *urine* and very little *sweating*.
7) It can tolerate *big changes* in its own *body temperature* to remove the need for sweating.

The Lion — a perfect Predator

1) *Strong jaws* and *sharp teeth* for killing prey.
2) Good *stereo vision* with both eyes *facing forwards*.
3) *Camouflaged body* for stalking.
4) *Strong*, *agile* and *fast*.
5) The right sort of *teeth* for *chewing meat*.

The Rabbit — a perfect Prey

1) *Fast* and *agile* for escaping capture.
2) Eyes on sides for *all-round vision*.
3) *Big ears* for good hearing.
4) *Brown colour* for *camouflage*.
5) *White tail* to alert pals.

Populations of Prey and Predators go in Cycles

In a community containing prey and predators (as most of them do of course):

1) The *POPULATION* of any species is usually *limited* by the amount of *FOOD* available.
2) If the population of the *PREY* increases, then so will the population of the *PREDATORS*.
3) However as the population of predators *INCREASES*, the number of prey will *DECREASE*.

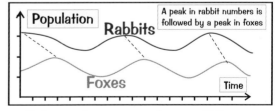

A peak in rabbit numbers is followed by a peak in foxes

i.e. *More grass* means *more rabbits*. More rabbits means *more foxes*. But more foxes means fewer *rabbits*.
Eventually fewer rabbits will mean *fewer foxes again*. This *up and down pattern* continues...

Creature features — learn and survive...

It's worth learning all these survival features well enough to be able to write them down *from memory*.
There's a whole world full of animals and plants, all with different survival features, but explaining them eventually becomes kinda "common sense", because the same principles tend to apply to them all.

Food Webs

A Woodland Food Web

Food webs are pretty easy really. Hideously easy in fact.

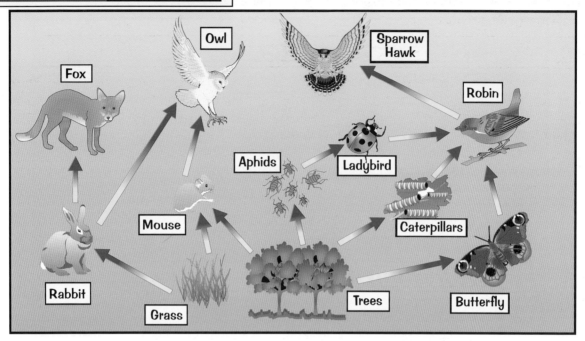

Food Chains — the Arrows show where the Energy goes

1) A _food chain_ is just part of a _food web_, starting at the bottom and _following the arrows_ up.
2) Remember, the _arrows_ show which way the _food energy travels_.
3) Don't mix up _who eats who_ either!
   The arrow means _"IS EATEN BY"_, so you _follow the arrow_ to the one doing the _eating_.
4) From the woodland food web we could take this _food chain_:

Terminology you need to know

1) _PRODUCER_ — all _plants_ are _producers_. They use the Sun's energy to produce food energy.
2) _HERBIVORE_ — animals which _only eat plants_, e.g. rabbits, caterpillars, aphids.
3) _CONSUMER_ — all _animals_ are _consumers_. All _plants_ are _not_, because they are producers.
4) _PRIMARY CONSUMER_ — animal which eats _producers_ (plants).
5) _SECONDARY CONSUMER_ — animal which eats primary consumers.
6) _CARNIVORE_ — eats _only animals_, never plants.
7) _TOP CARNIVORE_ — is _not eaten by anything else_, except decomposers after it dies.
8) _OMNIVORE_ — eats _both plants and animals_.
9) _DECOMPOSER_ — lives off all _dead material_ — producers, consumers, top carnivore, the lot.

Learn about Food Webs, terminology and all...

That's got to be the prettiest food web ever drawn, wouldn't you say? Yeah well, anyway, the pretty pictures are the easy bit. It's those _9 definitions_ which you really need to work at. That's what'll sort out the sheep from the goats in the Exam. So make sure you _know them all_.

Making Holes in Food Webs

A Typical Food Web for a Pond

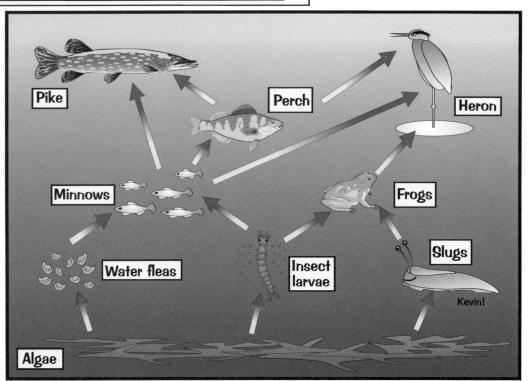

Pike · Perch · Heron · Minnows · Frogs · Water fleas · Insect larvae · Slugs · Kevin! · Algae

Exam Q. — What happens if you take out the frogs...?

1) This is the _usual Exam question_.
2) One of the animals is _wiped out_ — what effect will this have on the _other_ creatures?
3) For example, if all the _frogs_ were _removed_ what'd happen to the number of _slugs_ or _perch_?
4) It's _simple enough_, but you do have to _think it through_ fairly carefully:
   a) _SLUGS_ would _increase_ because there'd be _nothing to eat them_ now.
   b) _PERCH_ is a bit trickier. With no frogs the herons will get _hungry_ and so will _eat more perch_ (and minnows and insect larvae), so the perch will in fact _decrease_ in number.

You just have to understand the diagrams (i.e. who eats who) and think about it _real carefully_. Think about which animals _won't now get eaten_, and which animals _will go hungry_, and work out _what they'll do about it_ — and the effect that will have _on all the other things_ in the web.

Another Exam Q. — What if you took out the Minnows...?

1) First of all, _water fleas_ would _increase_.
2) _Perch_ on the other hand would be _really struggling_. They'd get _hungry_ for a start, but they'd also get _eaten_ a lot more _by pike_ and _heron_. Toughsky.
3) _Frogs_ would initially _benefit_ from _more insect larvae_ all to themselves, but would then suffer from _heron_ eating _more frogs_ due to there being _no minnows_ and fewer _perch_.
4) _Slugs_ would therefore _benefit_ because the _frogs_ would be eating more _insect larvae_ (instead of slugs) and also _getting eaten_ by heron. It's all real simple if you just _think it out_.

Learn about making holes in Food webs...

If they give you a food web question you can bet your very last fruit cake they're gonna want to wipe out one of the creatures and ask you what happens then. Practise with both these food webs by wiping out organisms (only one at a time!) and deciding what'll happen to the others.

Pyramids Of Number & Biomass

This is hideously easy too. Just _make sure you know_ what _all_ the pyramids mean.

Each Level you go up, there's fewer of them...

_5000_ dandelions... feed.. _100_ rabbits... which feed.... _one_ fox.

IN OTHER WORDS, each time you go _up one level_ the _number of organisms goes down_ — _A LOT_.
It takes _a lot_ of food from the level _below_ to keep any one animal alive.
This gives us the good old _number pyramid_:

| 1 Fox |
| 100 Rabbits |
| 5,000 Dandelions |

A typical pyramid of numbers

This is the _basic idea_ anyway. But there are cases where the pyramid is _not a pyramid at all_:

Number Pyramids Sometimes Look Wrong

This is a _pyramid_ except for the _top layer_ which goes _huge_:

| 500 Fleas |
| 1 Fox |
| 100 Rabbits |
| 5,000 Dandelions |

This is a _pyramid_ apart from the _bottom layer_ which is _way too small_:

| 1 Partridge |
| 1000 Ladybirds |
| 3,000 Aphids |
| 1 Pear tree |

Biomass Pyramids Never Look Wrong

When _number pyramids_ seem to go _wrong_ like this, then the good old _PYRAMID OF BIOMASS_
comes to the rescue. _Biomass_ is just how much all the creatures at each level would "_weigh_" if
you _put them all together_. So the _one pear tree_ would have a _big biomass_ and the _hundreds of
fleas_ would have _a very small biomass_. Biomass pyramids are _ALWAYS the right shape_:

| Fleas |
| Fox |
| Rabbits |
| Dandelions |

| Partridge |
| Ladybirds |
| Aphids |
| Pear tree |

Basically, _biomass pyramids_ are the only _sensible_ way to do it — it's just that _number pyramids_
are _easier to understand_.

Now Children, get your coloured wooden blocks out...

...hideously easy...

Energy Transfer & Efficient Food

All that Energy just Disappears Somehow...

1) Energy from the _SUN_ is the _source of energy_ for _all life on Earth_.

2) _Plants_ convert _a small %_ of the light energy that falls on them _into glucose_. This _energy_ then works its way through the _food web_.

3) The _ENERGY lost_ at each stage is used for _staying alive_, i.e. in _respiration_, which powers _all life processes_, including _movement_.

At each stage of the food chain material and energy are lost.

This explains why you get _biomass pyramids_. Most of the biomass is lost and so does _not_ become biomass in the _next level up_.

HEAT LOSS

MATERIALS LOST IN ANIMAL'S WASTE

4) Most of this energy is eventually _lost to the surroundings_ as _heat_. This is especially true for _mammals and birds_ whose bodies must be kept at a _constant temperature_ which is normally higher than their surroundings.

5) _Material and energy_ is also lost from the food chain in the _droppings_ — they burn when dried, proving they still have chemical energy in them.

Try it next time you're camping — you'll find you enjoy your midnight sausages that much more when cooked over a blazing mound of dried sheep poo.

Two Ways to Improve the "Efficiency" of Food Production

1) Reducing the Number of Stages in Food Chains

1) _For a given area of land_, you can produce _a lot more food_ (for humans) by growing _crops_ rather than by _grazing animals_. This is because you are reducing the number of stages in the food chain. Only _10%_ of what beef cattle eat becomes useful meat for people to eat.

2) However, don't forget that just eating _crops_ can quickly lead to _malnutrition_ through lack of essential _proteins_ and _minerals_, unless a varied enough diet is achieved. Also remember that _some land is unsuitable for growing crops_ like _moorland_ or _fellsides_. In these places, animals like _sheep_ and _deer_ are often the _best_ way to get food from the land.

2) Restricting the Energy Lost by Farm Animals

1) In 'civilised' countries such as ours, animals like _pigs_ and _chickens_ are reared in strict conditions of _limited movement_ and _artificial warmth_, in order to reduce their _energy losses_ to a minimum.

2) In other words keep them _still enough_ and _hot enough_ and they won't need _feeding as much_. It's as _simple_ and as _horrible_ as that. If you deny them even the simplest of simple pleasures in their short little stay on this planet before you eat them, then it won't cost you as much in feed. Lovely.

3) But _intensively reared_ animals like chickens and pigs, kept in a little shed all their life, _still require land indirectly_ because they still need _feeding_, so land is needed to _grow_ their "feed" on.
So would it be _so terrible_ to let them have a little corner of it in the sunshine somewhere, huh...?

Locked up in a little cage with no sunlight — who'd work in a bank...

Phew! Just look at all those words crammed onto one page. Geesh.... I mean blimey, it almost looks like a page from a normal science book. Almost. Anyway, there it all is, on the page, just waiting to be blended with the infinite void inside your head. _Learn and enjoy... and scribble._

Decomposition & the Carbon Cycle

Another sixties pop group? Sadly not.

1) *Living things* are made of *materials* they take from the world around them.
2) When they *decompose*, ashes are returned to ashes, and dust to dust, as it were.
3) In other words *the elements they contain* are returned to the *soil* where they came from *originally*.
4) These elements are then *used by plants* to grow and the whole cycle *repeats* over and over again.

Decomposition is carried out by Bacteria and Fungi

1) All *plant matter* and *dead animals* are broken down (digested) by *microbes*.
2) This happens everywhere in *nature*, and also in *compost heaps* and *sewage works*.
3) All the important *elements* are thus *recycled*:
   Carbon, *Hydrogen*, *Oxygen* and *Nitrogen*.
4) The *ideal conditions* for creating *compost* are:
   a) *WARMTH*
   b) *MOISTURE*
   c) *OXYGEN (AIR)*
   d) *MICROBES* (i.e. *bacteria* and *fungi)*
   e) *ORGANIC MATTER* cut into *small pieces*.
   Make sure you *learn them* — *ALL FIVE*.

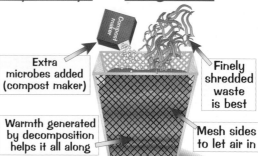

Extra microbes added (compost maker)

Finely shredded waste is best

Warmth generated by decomposition helps it all along

Mesh sides to let air in

There's a kid I know, and everyone calls him "the party mushroom". I'm not sure why really — they just say he's a fun guy to be with...

The Carbon Cycle Shows how Carbon is Recycled

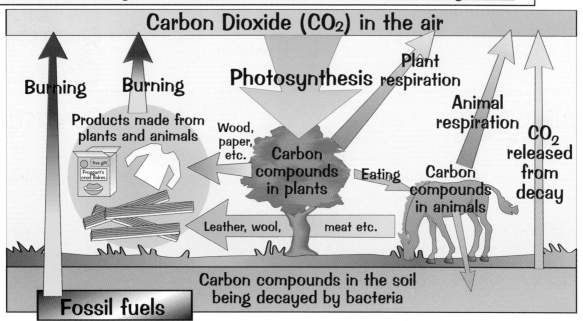

Carbon Dioxide (CO_2) in the air

Burning   Burning   Photosynthesis   Plant respiration   Animal respiration CO_2 released from decay

Products made from plants and animals

Wood, paper, etc.

Carbon compounds in plants

Eating

Carbon compounds in animals

Leather, wool,   meat etc.

Fossil fuels

Carbon compounds in the soil being decayed by bacteria

This diagram isn't half as bad as it looks. *LEARN* these important points:
1) There's only *one arrow* going *DOWN*. The whole thing is "powered" by *photosynthesis*.
2) Both plant and animal *respiration* puts CO_2 *back into the atmosphere*.
3) *Plants* convert the carbon in CO_2 *from the air* into *fats*, *carbohydrates* and *proteins*.
4) These can then go *three ways*: *be eaten*, *decay* or be turned into *useful products* by man.
5) *Eating* transfers some of the fats, proteins and carbohydrates to *new* fats, carbohydrates and proteins *in the animal* doing the eating.
6) Ultimately these plant and animal products either *decay* or are *burned* and CO_2 *is released*.

On Ilkley Moor ba 'tat, On Ilkley Moor ba 'tat...

...where the dogs play football...

Learn the five ideal conditions for compost making. They like asking about that.
Sketch out your *own simplified version* of the carbon cycle, making sure it contains all the labels.
Practise *scribbling* it out *from memory*. And *keep trying till you can*.

The Nitrogen Cycle

The _constant cycling_ of nitrogen through the atmosphere, soil and living organisms is called the _nitrogen cycle_.

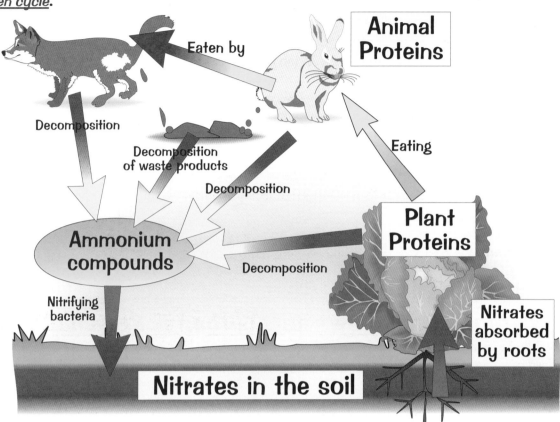

Animal Proteins

Eaten by

Decomposition

Decomposition of waste products

Decomposition

Eating

Plant Proteins

Decomposition

Ammonium compounds

Nitrifying bacteria

Nitrates absorbed by roots

Nitrates in the soil

There are Five Simple Stages to Learn

1) _Green plants_ absorb nitrogen in the form of _nitrates_ from the soil. _Nitrogen_ is an _important element_ in making _proteins_ for plants and animals.

2) _Animals_ can't use nitrogen directly and so must therefore _eat the plants_ to obtain it. Of course other animals then eat these animals to get their nitrogen.

3) _Any organic waste_, i.e. rotting plants or dead animals or animal poo, is broken down by _microbes_ into _ammonium compounds_. By the time the microbes and other organisms that break down this decaying matter have finished, almost _all the energy_ originally captured by the green plants has been _recycled_. Organisms such as the microbes, that do this decomposing job, are called _detritus feeders_. Detritus is simply the name given to all the decaying matter.

4) _Nitrifying bacteria_ turn the _ammonium compounds_ produced by the microbes into _useful nitrates_.

5) These _nitrates_ can then once more be absorbed by the roots of _green plants_.

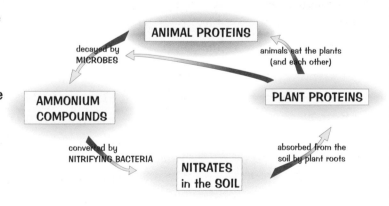

ANIMAL PROTEINS

decayed by MICROBES

animals eat the plants (and each other)

AMMONIUM COMPOUNDS

PLANT PROTEINS

converted by NITRIFYING BACTERIA

absorbed from the soil by plant roots

NITRATES in the SOIL

By Gum, you young 'uns have some stuff to learn...

It's really "grisly grimsdike" is the Nitrogen Cycle, I think. But the fun guys at the Exam Board want you to know all about it, so there you go. _Have a good time... and smile!_ ☺

There's Too Many People

There's one born every minute — and it's too many

1) The _population of the world_ is currently _rising out of control_ as the graph shows.

2) This is mostly due to _modern medicine_ which has stopped widespread death from _disease_.

3) It's also due to _modern farming methods_ which can now provide the _food_ needed for so many hungry mouths.

4) The _death rate_ is now _much lower_ than the _birth rate_ in many under-developed countries.
   In other words there are _lots more babies born_ than people _dying_.

5) This creates _big problems_ for those countries trying to cope with all those extra people.

6) Even providing _basic health care_ and _education_ (about contraception!) is difficult, never mind finding them _places to live_, and _food to eat_.

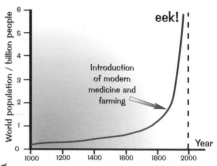

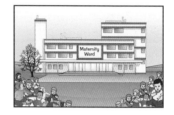

Increasing living Standards Adds Even More Pressure

The rapidly increasing population is not the only pressure on the environment. The _increasing standard of living_ amongst more _developed countries_ also demands more from the environment. These _two_ factors mean that:

1) Raw materials, including _non-renewable energy resources_, are rapidly being used up;

2) _more and more waste_ is being produced;

3) unless waste is properly handled _more pollution_ will be caused.

When the Earth's population was much smaller, the effects of human activity were usually small and local.

More People Means Less Land for Plants and Animals

There are _four_ main ways that humans _reduce_ the amount of land available for other _animals_ and _plants_.

1) _Building_

2) _Farming_

3) _Dumping Waste_

4) _Quarrying_

More People Means More Environmental Damage

Human activity can pollute all three parts of the environment:

1) _Water_ – with sewage, fertiliser and toxic chemicals;

2) _Air_ – with smoke and gases such as sulphur dioxide;

3) _Land_ – with toxic chemicals, such as pesticides and herbicides.
   These may then be washed from the land into water.

Learn the facts first — then you can build your rocket...

It's real scary innit — the way that graph of world population seems to be pointing nearly vertically upwards... tricky. Anyway, you just worry about your Exams instead, and make sure you learn all the grim facts. Four sections — _mini-essays_ for each, _till you know it all_.

Problems Caused By Farming

Farming Produces a Lot of Food, Which is Great but...

1) Farming is important to us because it allows us to produce _a lot of food_ from _less and less land_.

2) These days it has become quite a _high-tech_ industry. Food production is _big business_.

3) The great advantage of this is a _huge variety_ of _top quality_ foods, _all year round_, at _cheap prices_.

4) This is a far cry from Britain _50 years ago_ when food had to be _rationed_ by the government because there simply _wasn't enough_ for everyone. That's hard to imagine today... but try...

Fertilisers Damage Lakes and Rivers — Eutrophication

1) _Fertilisers_ which contain _nitrates_ are essential to _modern farming_.

2) Without them crops wouldn't grow nearly so well, and _food yields_ would be _well down_.

3) This is because the crops take _nitrates_ out of the soil and these nitrates need to be _replaced_.

4) The _problems_ start if some of the _rich fertiliser_ finds its way into _rivers_ and _streams_.

5) This happens quite easily if _too much fertiliser_ is applied, especially if it rains soon afterwards.

6) The result is _EUTROPHICATION_, which basically means "_too much of a good thing_".
   (_Raw sewage_ pumped into rivers also causes _EUTROPHICATION_ by providing food for microbes.)

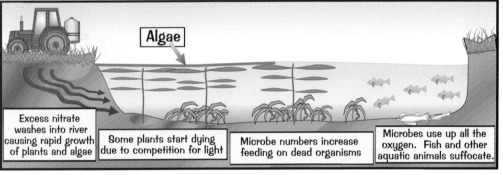

Algae

Excess nitrate washes into river causing rapid growth of plants and algae | Some plants start dying due to competition for light | Microbe numbers increase feeding on dead organisms | Microbes use up all the oxygen. Fish and other aquatic animals suffocate.

As the picture shows, _too many nitrates_ in the water cause a sequence of "_mega-growth_", "_mega-death_" and "_mega-decay_" involving most of the _plant_ and _animal life_ in the water.

7) _Farmers_ need to take _a lot more care_ when spreading _artificial fertilisers_.

Deforestation increases CO_2 Levels & the Greenhouse Effect

We have already pretty well deforested _OUR COUNTRY_. Now many _under-developed_ tropical countries are doing the same for timber and to provide land for agriculture. One of the main _environmental problems_ this causes is an _increase_ in the _greenhouse gas_, _carbon dioxide_ (CO_2). Deforestation increases CO_2 in the atmosphere in two ways:

1) The trees unsuitable for timber are _burned_ releasing CO_2 directly into the atmosphere.
   Microbes also release CO_2 by _decaying_ the felled trees that remain.

2) Because living trees use CO_2 for _photosynthesis_, removing these trees means _less_ CO_2 is removed from the atmosphere.

"There's nowt wrong wi' just spreadin' muck on it..."

Make sure you distinguish between _pesticides_ (which kill bugs) and _fertilisers_ (which supply nutrients to the plants). They can both cause harm but for totally different reasons. You have to learn the details carefully. _Mini-essay_ time again I'd say. _Cover the page and scribble..._

Greenhouse Effect & Acid Rain

Carbon Dioxide and Methane Trap Heat from the Sun

1) The _temperature_ of the Earth is a _balance_ between the heat it gets from the _Sun_ and the heat it _radiates back_ out into space.
2) The _atmosphere_ acts like an _insulating layer_ and keeps some of the heat _in_.
3) This is exactly what happens in _greenhouse_ or a _conservatory_. The sun shines into it and the glass keeps the heat in so it just gets _hotter and hotter_.
4) There are _several different gases_ in the atmosphere which are very good at _keeping the heat in_. They are called "_greenhouse gases_", oddly enough. The _main ones_ that we worry about are _methane_ and _carbon dioxide_, because the levels of these are _slowly rising_.
5) The _Greenhouse Effect_ is causing the Earth to _warm up_ very slowly.

The Greenhouse Effect may cause Flooding and Drought

1) An increase in the Earth's temperature of only a _few degrees_ Celsius could cause big changes in _weather patterns_ and _climate_ which may lead to _drought_ or _flooding_ in certain areas.
2) Higher temperatures could _melt_ the _polar ice-caps_ which would _raise sea-levels_ and could cause _flooding_ to many _low-lying_ coastal parts of the world including many _major cities_.

Methane is Also a Problem

1) _Methane gas_ is also contributing to the _Greenhouse Effect_.
2) It's produced _naturally_ from various sources, such as _natural marshland_.
3) However, the two sources of methane which are _on the increase_ are: a) _Rice growing_ b) _Cattle rearing_

Burning Fossil Fuels Causes Acid Rain

1) When _fossil fuels_ are _burned_ they release mostly _carbon dioxide_ which is causing the _Greenhouse Effect_ (see P. 10). They also release _two_ other _harmful gases_:
   a) _SULPHUR DIOXIDE_ b) various _NITROGEN OXIDES_
2) When these _mix with clouds_ they form _acids_. This then falls as _acid rain_.
3) _Cars_ and _power stations_ are the _main causes_ of acid rain.

Acid Rain Kills Fish, Trees and Statues

1) Acid rain causes _lakes_ to become _acidic_ which has a _severe effect_ on its _ecosystem_.
2) The way this happens is that the acid causes _aluminium salts_ to _dissolve_ into the water. The resulting _aluminium ions_ are _poisonous_ to many _fish and birds_.
3) Acid rain kills _trees_.
4) Acid rain _damages limestone buildings_ and _ruins stone statues_.

Learn the facts first — then start building your ark...

I bet you never realised there were so many drivelly details on the Greenhouse Effect and acid rain Well there _are_ and I'm afraid they could all come up in your Exam, so you just gotta learn them. Use the good old _mini-essay_ method for each section, and _scribble down what you know_...

Revision Summary for Module Three

There's a lot of words in Module Three. Most topics are pretty waffly with a lot of drivelly facts, and it can be real hard to learn them all. But learn them you must. You need to practise scribbling down what you can remember on each topic, and then checking back to see what you missed. These questions give you a pretty good idea of what you should know. You need to practise and practise them — till you can float through them all, like a cloud or something.

1) Name the four factors that affect individual organisms on a daily basis.
2) What are the *five* basic things which determine the size of a population of a species?
3) List seven survival features of the polar bear and of the camel.
5) Give five survival features for the lion and for the rabbit.
6) Sketch a graph of prey and predator populations and explain the shapes.
7) Describe what food chains and food webs are. Give two examples of both.
8) Write down the 9 technical terms about food webs (P.3) and give a definition of each one.
9) What is the basic approach to questions which make holes in food webs?
10) What are number pyramids? Why do you generally get a pyramid of numbers?
11) Why do number pyramids sometimes go wrong, and which pyramids are always right?
12) Where does the energy in a food chain originate? Name three ways in which the energy is lost.
13) Explain how might you improve the efficiency of food production?
14) Which two organisms are responsible for the decay of organic matter?
15) What are the five ideal conditions for making compost? Draw a compost maker.

16) What is the Carbon Cycle all to do with? Copy and fill in as much of it from memory as you can.
17) What is the Nitrogen Cycle all about? Draw as much of it from memory as you can.
18) Describe the five stages of the Nitrogen Cycle in as much detail as you can.
19) What is happening to the world's population? What is largely responsible for this trend?
20) What problems does a rapidly increasing population create for a country?
21) What are the four main ways humans reduce the land available for other plants and animals.
22) What effect does the ever-increasing number of people have on the environment?
23) What is the great bonus of modern farming methods? What are the drawbacks?
24) What happens when too much nitrate fertiliser is put onto fields? Give full details.
25) What is the big fancy name given to this problem? How can it be avoided?
26) How is deforestation linked to the greenhouse effect?
27) Which two gases are the biggest cause of the greenhouse effect?
28) Explain how the greenhouse effect happens. What dire consequences could there be?
29) What is causing the rise in levels of each the two problem gases. What is the solution?
30) Which gases cause acid rain? Where do these gases come from?
31) What are the three main harmful effects of acid rain? Explain exactly how fish are killed.
32) Give three ways that acid rain can be reduced.

Variation in Plants and Animals

1) Young plants and animals obviously _resemble_ their _parents_. In other words they show _similar characteristics_ such as jagged leaves or perfect eyebrows.

2) However young animals and plants can also _differ_ from their parents and each other.

3) These similarities and differences lead to _variation_ within the same species.

4) The word _"VARIATION"_ sounds far too fancy for its own good. All it means is how animals or plants of the same species _look or behave_ slightly different from each other. You know, a bit _taller_ or a bit _fatter_ or a bit more _scary-to-look-at_ etc.

There are _two_ causes of variation: _Genetic Variation_ and _Environmental Variation_.

Read on, and learn...

1) Genetic variation

You'll know this already.

1) _All animals_ (including humans) are bound to be _slightly different_ from each other because their _GENES_ are slightly different.

2) Genes are the code inside all your cells which determine how your body turns out. We all end up with a slightly different set of genes.

3) The _exceptions_ to that rule are _identical twins_, because their genes are _exactly the same_.

But even identical twins are never _completely identical_ — and that's because of the other factor:

2) Environmental Variation _is shown up by Twins_

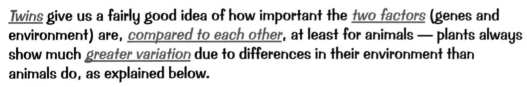

If you're not sure what _"environment"_ means, think of it as _"upbringing"_ instead — it's pretty much the same thing — how and where you were "brought up".

Since we know the _twins' genes_ are _identical_, any differences between them _must_ be caused by slight differences _in their environment_ throughout their lives.

Twins give us a fairly good idea of how important the _two factors_ (genes and environment) are, _compared to each other_, at least for animals — plants always show much _greater variation_ due to differences in their environment than animals do, as explained below.

Environmental _Variation in Plants is much Greater_

PLANTS are _strongly affected_ by:
1) _Temperature_
2) _Sunlight_
3) _Moisture level_
4) _Soil composition_

For example, plants may grow _twice as big_ or _twice as fast_ due to _fairly modest_ changes in environment such as the amount of _sunlight_ or _rainfall_ they're getting, or how _warm_ it is or what the _soil_ is like.

A cat, on the other hand, born and bred in the North of Scotland, could be sent out to live in equatorial Africa and would show no significant changes — it would look the same, eat the same, and it would probably still puke up everywhere.

Don't let Everything get to you — just learn the facts...

There are four sections on this page. After you think you've learnt it all, _cover the pages_ and do a "_mini-essay_" on each of the six sections. Then _check back_ and see what important points you missed.

14

Genes, Chromosomes and DNA

If you're going to get _anywhere_ with this topic you definitely need to learn these confusing words and exactly what they mean. You have to _make sure you know_ exactly what _DNA_ is, what and where _chromosomes_ are, and what and where a _gene_ is. If you don't get that sorted out first, then anything else you read about them won't make a lot of sense to you — _will it?_

any cell in your body

nucleus

The human cell nucleus contains _23 pairs of chromosomes_. They are all well known and numbered. We all have two No. 19 chromosomes and two No.12s etc.

A single _chromosome_

A _PAIR_ of _chromosomes_. (They're always in pairs, one from each parent.)

Short sections of a chromosome are called _GENES_. We know that certain sections of certain chromosomes do particular things, e.g. the hair colour gene.

A _gene_, a _short length_ of the chromosome...

DNA molecule

...which is quite a _long length_ of _DNA_.

The arms are held together in the centre

An _ALLELE_ is _another name for a gene_, so these sections of chromosome are also _alleles_. (When there are _two different versions_ of the same gene you call them _alleles_ instead of genes — it's more sensible than it sounds!)

The DNA is _coiled up_ to form the _arms_ of the _chromosome_.

Homozygous — is an individual with _two alleles the same_ for that particular gene, e.g. HH or hh.
Heterozygous — is an individual with _two alleles different_ for that particular gene, e.g. Hh.
Meiosis — is the process of _cell division_ which _creates sperm or egg cells_. Meiosis only happens in the _ovaries_ or the _testes_.
Mitosis — is the process of _cell division_ where one cell splits into _two identical cells_.
Gamete — is either a _sperm cell_ or an _egg cell_. All _gametes_ have half the number of chromosomes of a body cell.
Zygote — is the delightful name given to each newly-formed human life, just after the (equally delightfully-named) _gametes fuse together_ at fertilisation.

Hard Learning? — don't blow it all out of proportion...

This is a real easy page to learn, don't you think. Why, you could learn the whole thing with both ears tied behind your head. _Cover the page_ and _scribble down_ all the diagrams and details.

Ordinary Cell Division: Mitosis

> "*MITOSIS* is when a cell reproduces itself *ASEXUALLY* *by splitting* to form *two identical offspring* that are called *clones*."

The really riveting part of the whole process is how the chromosomes split inside the cell. Learn and enjoy...

DNA all spread out in *long strings*.

DNA forms into chromosomes. Remember, the *double arms* are already *duplicates* of each other.

Chromosomes line up along centre and then *the cell fibres pull them apart*.

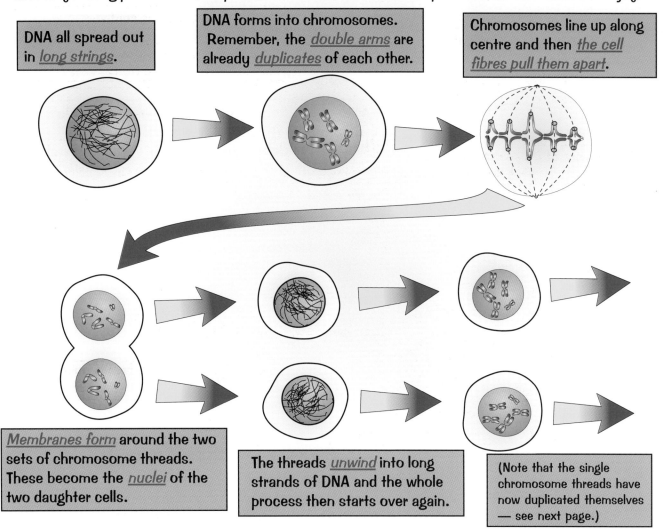

Membranes form around the two sets of chromosome threads. These become the *nuclei* of the two daughter cells.

The threads *unwind* into long strands of DNA and the whole process then starts over again.

(Note that the single chromosome threads have now duplicated themselves — see next page.)

Asexual Reproduction

ORDINARY CELL DIVISION produces new cells *identical* to the original cell. This is how all plants and animals *grow* and produce *replacement cells*. Cells throughout our body *divide* and *multiply* by this process. However some organisms also *reproduce* using ordinary cell division, *bacteria* being a good example. This is known as *asexual* reproduction. Here is a *DEFINITION* of it, for you to learn:

> In *ASEXUAL REPRODUCTION* there is only *ONE* parent, and the offspring therefore have *exactly the same genes* as the parent (i.e. they're clones — see P. 19).

This is because all the cells *in both parent and offspring* were produced by *ordinary cell division*, so they must all have *identical genes* in their cell nuclei. Asexual reproduction therefore produces no variation. Some *plants* reproduce asexually, e.g. potatoes, strawberries and daffodils (see P. 20).

Now that I have your undivided attention...

You need to *learn* the definition of *mitosis* and the sequence of diagrams, and also the definition of *asexual reproduction*. Now *cover the page* and *scribble down* the two definitions and sketch out the sequence of diagrams — *don't waste time* with neatness — just find out if you've *learnt it all* yet.

Gamete Production: Meiosis

You thought mitosis was exciting. Hah! You ain't seen nothing yet. _Meiosis_ is the other type of cell division. It only happens in the _reproductive organs_ (ovaries and testes).

> _MEIOSIS_ produces "_cells which have half the proper number of chromosomes_".
> Such cells are also known as "_gametes_".

These cells are "genetically different" from each other because _the genes all get shuffled up_ during meiosis and each gamete only gets _half of them_, selected at random.
Confused? I'm not surprised. But fear not, my little yellow friend...
The diagrams below will make it a lot clearer — but you have to _study_ them pretty hard.

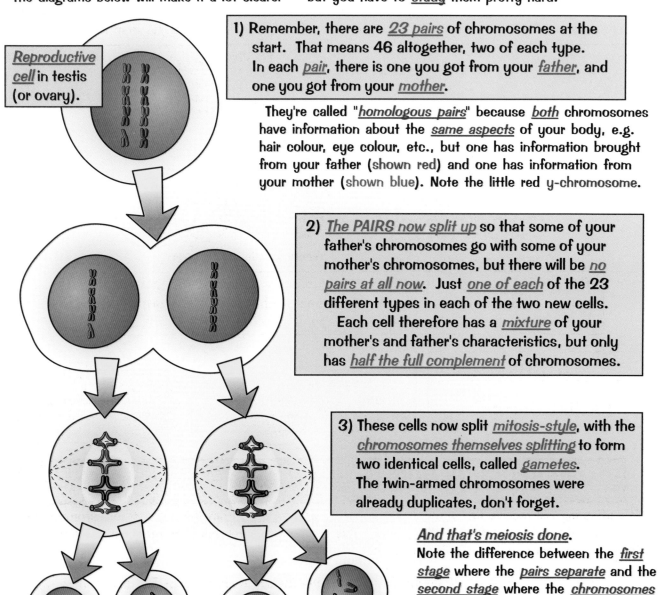

Reproductive cell in testis (or ovary).

1) Remember, there are _23 pairs_ of chromosomes at the start. That means 46 altogether, two of each type. In each _pair_, there is one you got from your _father_, and one you got from your _mother_.

They're called "_homologous pairs_" because _both_ chromosomes have information about the _same aspects_ of your body, e.g. hair colour, eye colour, etc., but one has information brought from your father (shown red) and one has information from your mother (shown blue). Note the little red y-chromosome.

2) _The PAIRS now split up_ so that some of your father's chromosomes go with some of your mother's chromosomes, but there will be _no pairs at all now_. Just _one of each_ of the 23 different types in each of the two new cells. Each cell therefore has a _mixture_ of your mother's and father's characteristics, but only has _half the full complement_ of chromosomes.

3) These cells now split _mitosis-style_, with the _chromosomes themselves splitting_ to form two identical cells, called _gametes_. The twin-armed chromosomes were already duplicates, don't forget.

And that's meiosis done.
Note the difference between the _first stage_ where the _pairs separate_ and the _second stage_ where the _chromosomes themselves split_. It's tricky!

GAMETES
i.e. sperm cells or (egg cells).

Meiosis? Not even remotely scary...

There's a few tricky words in there which don't help — especially if you just ignore them...
The only way to _learn_ this page is by constant reference to the diagram. Make sure you can sketch all the parts of it _from memory_ and _scribble notes_ to explain each stage. Even so, it's still difficult to understand it all, never mind remember it. But that's what you gotta do!

Fertilisation: Meeting of Gametes

There are 23 Pairs of Human Chromosomes

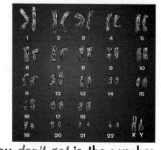

They are well known and numbered. In every _cell nucleus_ we have _two of each type_. The diagram shows the 23 pairs of chromosomes from a human cell. _One_ chromosome in _each pair_ is inherited from _each of our parents_. Normal body cells have 46 chromosomes, in _23 homologous pairs_.

Remember, "_homologous_" means that the two chromosomes in each pair are _equivalent_ to each other. In other words, the number 19 chromosomes from both your parents _pair off together_, as do the number 17s etc. What you _don't get_ is the number 12 chromosome from one parent pairing off with, say, the number 5 chromosome from the other.

Reproductive Cells _undergo_ Meiosis _to Produce_ Gametes:

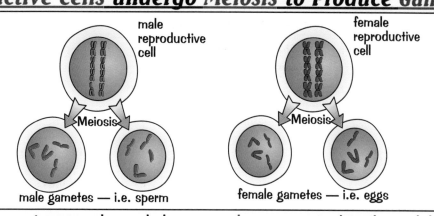

male reproductive cell

female reproductive cell

Meiosis

Meiosis

male gametes — i.e. sperm

female gametes — i.e. eggs

The _gametes_ remember, only have _one chromosome_ to describe each bit of you, _one copy_ of each of the chromosomes numbered 1 to 23. But a _normal cell_ needs _two_ chromosomes of each type — one from _each parent_, so...

Sexual Reproduction

Fertilisation:

sperm

Gametes

egg

Offspring

fertilised egg

SEXUAL REPRODUCTION involves the fusion of male and female gametes (sex cells). Because there are _TWO_ parents, the offspring contains _a mixture of their parents genes_.

The offspring will receive its _outward characteristics_ as a _mixture_ from the _two_ sets of chromosomes, so it will _inherit features_ from _both parents_. This is why _sexual_ reproduction produces more variation than _asexual_ reproduction. Pretty cool, eh.

WHEN THE GAMETES MEET UP during fertilisation, the 23 single chromosomes in one gamete _will all pair off_ with their appropriate "partner chromosomes" from the other gamete to form the full 23 pairs again, No.4 with No.4, No.13 with No.13 etc. etc.

Don't forget, the two chromosomes in a pair _both contain the same basic genes_, e.g. for hair colour, etc. When single chromosomes _meet up_ at fertilisation, they _seek out_ their counterpart from the other gamete.

It should all be starting to come together now...

If you go through these last two pages you should see how the two processes, meiosis and fertilisation, are kind of opposite. Practise _sketching out_ the sequence of diagrams, with notes, for both pages till it all sinks in. Nice, innit.

Selective Breeding

Selective Breeding *is Very Simple*

SELECTIVE BREEDING is also called _artificial selection_, because humans artificially select the plants or animals that are going to breed and flourish, according to what _WE_ want from them.

This is the basic process involved in selective breeding:

1) From your existing stock select the ones which have the _BEST CHARACTERISTICS_.
2) _Breed them_ with each other.
3) Select the _best_ of the _OFFSPRING_, and combine them with the best that you already have and _breed again_.
4) Continue this process over _SEVERAL GENERATIONS_ to _develop_ the _desired traits_.

Selective Breeding is *Very Useful* in Farming

Artificial Selection like this is used in _most areas of modern farming_, to great benefit:

1) *Better BEEF*

Selectively breeding _beef cattle_ to get the _best beef_ (taste, texture, appearance, etc.).

2) *Better MILK*

Selectively breeding _milking cows_ to increase _milk yield_ and _resistance to disease_.

3) *Better CHICKENS*

Selectively breeding _chickens_ to improve _egg size_ and _number_ of eggs per hen.

4) *Better WHEAT*

Selectively breeding _wheat_ to produce new varieties with better _yields_ and better _disease-resistance_ too.

5) *Better FLOWERS*

Selectively breeding _flowers_ to produce _bigger_ and _better_ and _more colourful ones_.

The Main Drawback *is a Reduction in the Gene Pool*

In farming, animals are selectively bred to develop the best features, which are basically:

A) _MAXIMUM YIELD_ of meat, milk, grain etc.
B) _GOOD HEALTH_ and _DISEASE RESISTANCE_.

1) But selective breeding reduces the _number of alleles_ in a population because the farmer keeps breeding from the "best" animals or plants — the same ones all the time.
2) This can cause serious problems if a _new disease appears_, as all the plants or animals could be wiped out.
3) This is made more likely because all the stock are _closely related_ to each other, so if one of them is going to be killed by a new disease, the others are also likely to succumb to it.

Oh Eck!

| Selective Breeding | → | Reduction in the number of different alleles (genes) | → | Less chance of any resistant alleles being present in the population | → | Nothing to selectively breed a new strain from |

Don't sit there brooding over it, just learn the info...

Selective breeding is a very simple topic. In the Exam they'll likely give you half a page explaining how a farmer in Sussex did this or that with his crops or cows, and then they'll suddenly ask: "_What is meant by selective breeding_". That's when you just write down the four points at the top of the page. Then they'll ask you to "_Suggest other ways that selective breeding might be used by farmers in Sussex to improve their yield_". That's when you just list some of the examples that you've learnt.

Genetic Engineering & Cloning

Learn this *definition* of clones: **CLONES** are **GENETICALLY IDENTICAL ORGANISMS**

Clones occur *naturally* in both plants and animals. *Identical twins* are clones of each other.
These days clones are very much a part of the *high-tech farming industry*.

Embryo Transplants in Cows

Normally, farmers only breed from their *BEST* cows and bulls. However, such traditional methods would only allow the *prize cow* to produce *one new offspring each year*. These days the whole process has been transformed using *EMBRYO TRANSPLANTS*:

1) *SPERM* are taken from the prize bull.
2) They're checked for *genetic defects* and which *SEX* they are.
3) They can also be *FROZEN* and used at a later date.
4) Selected prize cows are given *HORMONES* to make them produce *LOTS OF EGGS*.
5) The cows are then *ARTIFICIALLY INSEMINATED*.
6) *THE EMBRYOS* are taken from prize cows and checked for sex and genetic defects.
7) The embryos are developed and *SPLIT* (to form *CLONES*) before any cells become specialised.
8) These embryos are *IMPLANTED* into other cows, where they grow. They can also be *FROZEN* and used at a later date.

"Nurse — the screens!"

ADVANTAGES OF EMBRYO TRANSPLANTS — *Hundreds of Ideal Offspring*

a) *Hundreds* of "ideal" offspring can be produced *every year* from the best bull and cow.
b) The original prize cow can keep producing *prize eggs all year round*.

DISADVANTAGES — *Reduced Gene Pool*

Only the *usual drawback with clones* — a reduced *"gene pool"* leading to *vulnerability to new diseases*.

Genetic Engineering is Ace — hopefully

This is a new science with exciting possibilities, but *dangers* too. The basic idea is to move sections of *DNA* (genes) from one organism to another so that it produces *useful biological products*. We presently use bacteria to produce *human insulin* for diabetes sufferers and also to produce *human growth hormone* for children who aren't growing properly.

Genetic Engineering involves these Important Stages:

1) The useful gene is *"CUT"* from the DNA of say a human.
2) This is done using *ENZYMES*. Particular enzymes will cut out particular bits of DNA.
3) *ENZYMES* are then used to *cut the DNA* of a *bacterium* and the human gene is then inserted.
4) Again this *"SPLICING"* of a new gene is controlled by certain *specific enzymes*.
5) The bacterium is now *CULTIVATED* and soon there are *millions* of similar bacteria all producing, say human insulin.
6) This can be done on an *INDUSTRIAL SCALE* and the useful product can be *separated out*.
7) The same approach can also be used to *transfer useful genes into ANIMAL EMBRYOS*. Sheep for example can be developed which produce useful substances (i.e. drugs) in *their milk!* This is a very easy way to produce drugs...

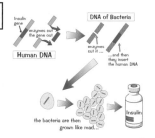

Insulin gene — enzymes cut the gene out — Human DNA

DNA of Bacteria — enzymes cut it ... — ...and then they insert the human DNA

the bacteria are then grown like mad... — Insulin

Hmmph... Kids these days, they're all the same...

Once again, they could ask you about any of the details on this page. The only way to be sure you know it: *cover the page* and write *mini-essays* on both topics. Then see what you missed, and *try again*...

Cloned Plants

Many Plants Produce Clones — all by themselves

This means they produce _exact genetic copies_ of themselves _without involving another plant_.
Here are three common ones:

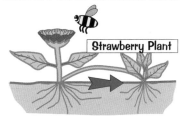 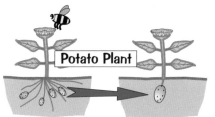 

1) _STRAWBERRY PLANTS_ producing _runners_.

2) New _POTATO PLANTS_ growing from tubers of old plant.

3) _Bulbs_ such as _DAFFODILS_ growing new bulbs off the side of them.

Gardeners Make Clones from Cuttings

1) Gardeners are familiar with taking _cuttings_ from good parent plants, and then planting them to produce _identical copies_ (clones) of the parent plant.

2) The cuttings are kept in a _damp atmosphere_ until their _roots develop_.

3) These plants can be produced _quickly and cheaply_.

4) These days, this basic technique has been given the _full high-tech treatment_ by _commercial plant breeders_:

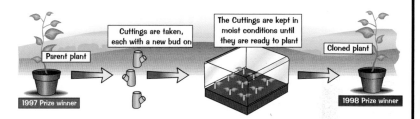

The Essentials of Commercial Cloning:

TISSUE CULTURE

This is where, instead of starting with at least a stem and bud, they just put _A FEW PLANT CELLS_ in a _growth medium_ with _hormones_ and it just grows into _A NEW PLANT_. Just like that! Phew.

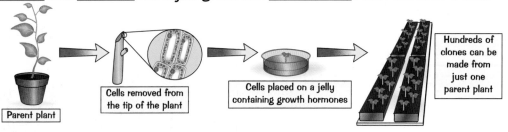

ADVANTAGES OF TISSUE CULTURE:

1) Very _FAST_ — can produce thousands of plantlets in a few weeks.
2) Very little _SPACE_ needed.
3) _CAN GROW ALL YEAR_ — no problem with weather or seasons.
4) New plants are _DISEASE-FREE_.
5) _NEW PLANTS_ can be _DEVELOPED_ (very quickly) by splicing new genes into plantlets and seeing how they turn out.

DISADVANTAGES OF TISSUE CULTURE:

Only the usual drawback with clones — _a reduced "gene pool"_ leading to _vulnerability to new diseases_.

Stop Cloning Around and just learn it...

I hope you realise that they could easily test your knowledge of _any_ sentence on this page. I only put in stuff you need to know, you know. Practise scribbling out all the facts on this page, _mini-essay style_.

Fossils

FOSSILS are the _"remains"_ of plants and animals which lived _millions of years ago_.

There are Three ways that Fossils can be Formed:

1) FROM THE _HARD PARTS_ OF ANIMALS   (Most fossils happen this way.)

Things like _bones_, _teeth_, _shells_, etc., which _don't decay_ easily, can last a long time when _buried_. They're eventually _replaced by minerals_ as they decay, forming a _rock-like substance_ shaped like the original hard part. The surrounding sediments also turn to rock, but the fossil stays _distinct_ inside the rock, and eventually someone _digs it up_.

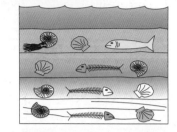

2) FROM THE _SOFTER PARTS_ OF ANIMALS OR PLANTS — _PETRIFICATION_

Sometimes fossils are formed from the _softer parts_ which somehow haven't decayed. The soft material gradually becomes _"petrified"_ (turns to stone) as it slowly decays and is _replaced by minerals_. This is _rare_, since there are _very few occasions_ when decay occurs so _slowly_.

buried leaf

replaced by minerals

3) IN PLACES WHERE _NO DECAY_ HAPPENS

The _whole original plant or animal_ may survive for _thousands of years_:

a) _AMBER_ — no _OXYGEN_ or _MOISTURE_ for the _decay microbes_.

INSECTS are often found _fully preserved_ in amber, which is a clear yellow "stone" made of _FOSSILISED RESIN_ that ran out of an ancient tree hundreds of millions of years ago, engulfing the insect.

b) _GLACIERS_ — too _COLD_ for the _decay microbes_ to work.

A _HAIRY MAMMOTH_ was found fully preserved in a glacier somewhere several years ago.

(at least that's what I heard, though I never saw any pictures of it so maybe it was a hoax, I'm not really sure, but anyway in principle one could turn up any time...)

c) _WATERLOGGED BOGS_ — too _ACIDIC_ for _decay microbes_.

A _10,000 year old man_ was found in a bog a few years ago. He was dead, and a bit squashed but otherwise quite well preserved, although it was clear he had been murdered.

(Police are not looking for any witnesses and have asked anyone _else_ who thinks they may have important information to just keep away.)

Evidence from Rock and Soil Strata

The fossils found in _rock layers_ tell us _TWO THINGS_:

1) What the creatures and plants _LOOKED LIKE_.
2) _HOW LONG AGO THEY EXISTED_, by the type of rock they're in. Generally speaking, the _DEEPER_ you find the fossil, the _OLDER_ it will be, though of course rocks get pushed upwards and eroded, so very old rocks can become exposed.

Fossils are usually _dated_ by geologists who _ALREADY KNOW THE AGE OF THE ROCK_. The Grand Canyon in Arizona is about _1 mile deep_. It was formed by a river slowly cutting down through layers of rock. The rocks at the bottom are about _1,000,000,000 years old_, and the fossil record in the sides is pretty cool.

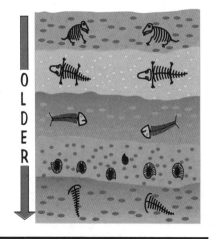

O
L
D
E
R

Don't get bogged down in all this information...

Make sure you're fully aware of the _three_ different types of _fossil_ and how they're _formed_. Also make sure you learn all the details about what information rocks provide. Many people read stuff and then think they know it. It's only if you _cover it up_ that you find out what you _really_ know.

Evolution

The Theory of Evolution is Cool

1) This suggests that all the animals and plants on Earth gradually "_evolved_" over _millions of years_, rather than just suddenly popping into existence. Makes sense.

2) Life on Earth began as _simple organisms living in water_ and gradually everything else evolved from there. And it only took about _3,000,000,000 years_.

Fossils Provide Evidence for it

1) _Fossils_ provide lots of _evidence_ for evolution.
2) They show how today's species have _changed and developed_ over _millions of years_.
3) There are quite a few "_missing links_" though because the fossil record is _incomplete_.
4) This is because _very very few_ dead plants or animals actually turn into fossils.
5) Most just _decay away_ completely.

The Evolution of The Horse is Ace

1) One set of fossils which _is_ pretty good though is that showing _the evolution of the horse_.
2) This developed from quite a small creature about the size of a _dog_ and the fossils show how the _middle toe_ slowly became bigger and bigger and eventually evolved into the familiar _hoof_ of today's horse.
3) It took about _60 million years_ though.
4) This is _pretty strong evidence_ in support of _evolution_ because it really shows evolution happening!

Forefeet   Evolution of the horse

Hyracotherium

Mesohippus

Merychippus

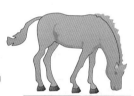

Pliohippus

Modern

Extinction is Pretty Bad News

The _dinosaurs_ and _hairy mammoths_ became _EXTINCT_ and it's only _FOSSILS_ that tell us they ever existed at all, (notwithstanding the odd questionable glacier story).

There are _THREE WAYS_ a species can become _EXTINCT_:
1) The _ENVIRONMENT CHANGES_ too quickly.
2) A new _PREDATOR_ or _DISEASE_ kills them all.
3) They can't _COMPETE_ with another (new) species for _FOOD_.

As the environment _slowly changes_, it will gradually favour certain new characteristics amongst the members of the species and over many generations those features will _proliferate_. In this way, the species _constantly adapts_ to its changing environment. But if the environment changes _too fast_ the whole species may be _wiped out_, i.e. _extinction_...

Stop horsing around and just learn the facts...

Another stupefyingly easy page to learn. Use the _mini-essay_ method. Just make sure you _learn every fact_, that's all. Dinosaurs never did proper revision and look what happened to them. (Mind you they did last about 200 million years, which is about 199.9 million more than we have, so far...)

Natural Selection

Darwin's Theory of Natural Selection is Ace

1) _THIS THEORY IS COOL_ and provides _a comprehensive explanation for all life on Earth_.

2) Mind you, it caused some trouble at the time, because for the first time ever, there was a highly plausible explanation for our own existence, without the need for a "Creator".

3) This was _bad news_ for the religious authorities of the time, who tried to ridicule old Charlie's ideas. But, as they say, _"THE TRUTH WILL OUT"_.

Darwin made Four Important Observations...

1) All organisms produce _MORE OFFSPRING_ than could possibly survive.

2) But in fact, population numbers tend to remain _FAIRLY CONSTANT_ over long periods of time.

3) Organisms in a species show _WIDE VARIATION_ due to different genes.

4) _SOME_ of the variations are _INHERITED AND PASSED ON_ to the next generation.

...and then made these Two Deductions:

1) Since most offspring don't survive, all organisms must have to _STRUGGLE FOR SURVIVAL_. (_Predation_, _disease_ and _competition_ cause large numbers of individuals to die).

2) The ones who _SURVIVE AND REPRODUCE_ will _PASS ON THEIR GENES_.

This is the famous _"SURVIVAL OF THE FITTEST"_ statement. Organisms with slightly less survival-value will probably perish first, leaving the _strongest and fittest_ to _pass on their genes_ to the next generation.

Mutations play a big part in Natural Selection...

...by creating a _new feature_ with a _high survival value_. Once upon a time maybe all rabbits had _short ears_ and managed OK. Then one day out popped a mutant with _BIG EARS_ who was always the first to dive for cover. Pretty soon he's got a whole family of them with _BIG EARS_, all diving for cover before the other rabbits, and before you know it there's only _BIG-EARED_ rabbits left because the rest just didn't hear trouble coming quick enough.
(_Eat your heart out, Rudyard Kipling_)

FOX!

A Modern Example — Flat Cockroaches

A creepy crawly example of _evolution_ is all too apparent in many kitchens around the world.

1) As health inspectors wage war on them, little do they realise how much the _cockroach_ has gone out of its way to fit in.

2) Over the centuries, as man and cockroaches have _shared accommodation_ the cockroaches have actually become _smaller and flatter_ to adapt to our domestic environment.

3) In each generation the smaller, flatter offspring find _easier access_ to our larders and _more places to hide_, while the _larger_, _bulkier_ offspring get squashed out.

I knew I should have lost a few pounds...

"Natural Selection" — sounds like Vegan Chocolates...

This page is split into five sections. _Memorise_ the headings, then _cover the page_ and _scribble down_ all you can about each section. Keep trying until you can _remember_ all the important points.

X and Y Chromosomes

There are 23 matched pairs of chromosomes in every human body cell. You'll notice the 23rd pair are labelled XY. They're the two chromosomes that decide whether you turn out male or female. They're called the X and Y chromosomes because they look like an X and a Y.

> **ALL MEN** have _an X_ and _a Y_ chromosome: XY
> _The Y chromosome is DOMINANT_ and causes _male characteristics_.
>
> **ALL WOMEN** have _two X chromosomes_: XX
> The **XX** combination allows _female characteristics_ to develop.

The diagram below shows the way the male XY chromosomes and female XX chromosomes _split up to form the gametes_ (eggs or sperm), and then _combine together at fertilisation_.
  The criss cross lines show all the _possible_ ways the X and Y chromosomes _could_ combine. Remember, _only one of these_ would actually happen for any offspring.
What the diagram shows us is the _RELATIVE PROBABILITY_ of each type of zygote (offspring) occurring.

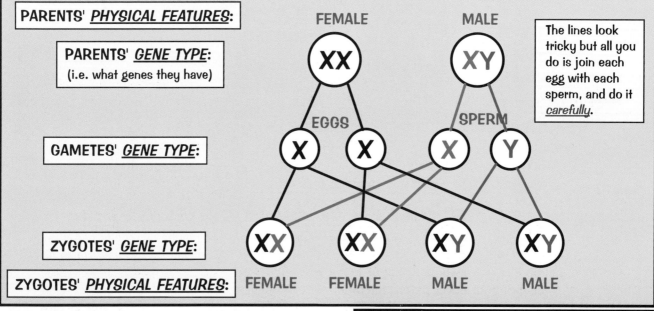

PARENTS' _PHYSICAL FEATURES_:

PARENTS' _GENE TYPE_:
(i.e. what genes they have)

GAMETES' _GENE TYPE_:

ZYGOTES' _GENE TYPE_:

ZYGOTES' _PHYSICAL FEATURES_: FEMALE   FEMALE   MALE   MALE

The lines look tricky but all you do is join each egg with each sperm, and do it carefully.

The other way of doing this is with a _checkerboard_ type diagram. If you don't understand how it works, ask "Teach" to explain it. The _pairs of letters_ in the middle show the _gene types_ of the possible offspring.

Both diagrams show that there'll be the _same proportion_ of _male and female offspring_, because there are _two XX results_ and _two XY results_.

Don't forget that this _50:50 ratio_ is only a _probability_. If you had four kids they _could_ all be _boys_ — yes I know, terrifying isn't it?

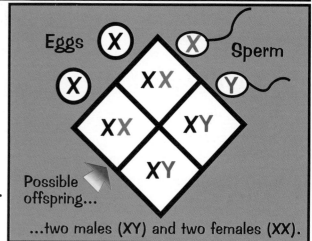

...two males (XY) and two females (XX).

How can it take all that just to say it's a 50:50 chance...

Make sure you know all about **X** and **Y** chromosomes and who has what combination.
The diagrams are real important. Practise reproducing them until you can do it _effortlessly_.

Breeding Terminology

Breeding Two Plants or Animals Who have One Gene Different

The best way to see what you get is with a diagram like either of these:

But first learn all these technical terms — it's real difficult to follow what's going on if you don't:

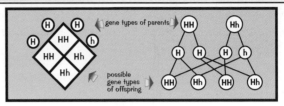

1) ALLELE
— this is just another name for a *GENE*. If you have *two different versions of a gene*, like H and h, then you have to call them *ALLELES* instead of genes.

2) DOMINANT AND RECESSIVE
— self explanatory. A dominant allele *DOMINATES* a recessive allele.

3) "PARENTAL", "F1" AND "F2" GENERATIONS
— pretty obvious. The two *originals* that you cross are the *parental generation*, their *kids* are the *F1 generation* and the *"grandchildren"* are the *F2 generation*. Easy peasy.

4) HOMOZYGOUS AND HETEROZYGOUS
— *"Homo-"* means *"same kinda things"*, *"Hetero-"* means *"different kinda things"*. They stick *"-zygous"* on the end to show we're talking about *genes*, (rather than any other aspect of Biology), and also just to make it *sound more complicated*, I'm certain of it. So...

"HOMOZYGOUS RECESSIVE" is the descriptive shorthand (hah!) for this:	hh
"HOMOZYGOUS DOMINANT" is the 'shorthand' for	HH
"HETEROZYGOUS" is the 'shorthand' for	Hh
"A HOMOZYGOTE" or *"A HETEROZYGOTE"* are how you refer to people with such genes.	

An Almost Unbearably Exciting Example

Let's take a *thoroughbred crazy hamster*, genotype hh, with a *thoroughbred normal hamster*, genotype HH, and cross breed them. You must learn this whole diagram thoroughly, till you can do it all yourself:

P1 Parents' *PHYSICAL TYPE*:   *Normal and boring*   *Wild and scratty*
P1 Parents' *GENE TYPE*:

Gametes' *GENE TYPE*:

F1 Zygotes' *GENE TYPE*:
F1 Zygotes' *PHYSICAL TYPE*:   *They're all normal and boring*

If two of these F1 generation now breed they will produce the F2 generation:

F1 Parents' *PHYSICAL TYPE*:   Normal and boring   Normal and boring
F1 Parents' *GENE TYPE*:

Gametes' *GENE TYPE*:

F2 Zygotes' *GENE TYPE*:
F2 Zygotes' *PHYSICAL TYPE*:   Normal   Normal   Normal   *CRAZY!*

This gives a *3 : 1 RATIO* of Normal to Crazy Offspring in the F2 generation. Remember that *"results"* like this are only *PROBABILITIES*. It doesn't mean it'll happen. (Most likely, you'll end up trying to contain a mini-riot of nine lunatic baby hamsters.)

See how those fancy words start to roll off the tongue...

The diagram and all its fancy words need to be second nature to you. So practise writing it out *from memory* until you get it all right. Because when you can do one — *you can do 'em all*.

26

Mutations

A MUTATION occurs when an organism develops with some _strange new characteristic_ that no other member of the species has had before. For example if someone was born with blue hair it would be caused by a mutation. Some mutations are beneficial, but _most are disastrous_ (e.g. blue hair).

Radiation and Certain Chemicals cause Mutations

Mutations occur 'naturally', probably caused by "natural" background radiation (from the sun, and rocks etc.) or just the laws of chance that every now and then the DNA doesn't quite copy itself properly. However _the chance of mutation is increased_ by exposing yourself:

1) to _ionising radiation_, including _X-rays_ and _Ultra-Violet light_, (which are the highest-frequency parts of the _EM spectrum_) together with radiation from _radioactive substances_. For each of these examples, the _greater_ the _dose_ of radiation, the _greater_ the _chance_ of mutation.

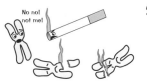

2) to certain _chemicals_ which are known to cause mutations. Such chemicals are called _mutagens_. If the mutations produce cancer then the chemicals are often called _carcinogens_. Cigarette smoke contains chemical mutagens (or carcinogens).

Mutations are Caused by Faults in the DNA

There are _several ways_ that mutations happen, but in the end they're all down to _faulty DNA_. Mutations _usually happen_ when the DNA is _replicating itself_ and something goes wrong. Because _DNA_ is what _genes_ are made of, and also what _chromosomes_ are made of, then there are several different _definitions_ of what a mutation is.
However this is the one in the syllabus and you should learn it:

> *A MUTATION* is a change to one or more genes.

Most Mutations are Harmful

1) If a mutation occurs in _reproductive cells_, then the young may _develop abnormally_ or _die_ at an early stage of their development.
2) If a mutation occurs in body cells, the mutant cells may start to _multiply_ in an _uncontrolled_ way and _invade_ other parts of the body. This is what we know as _CANCER_.

Some Mutations are Beneficial, giving us "EVOLUTION"

1) _Blue budgies_ appeared suddenly as a mutation amongst yellow budgies. This is a good example of a _neutral effect_. It didn't harm its chances of survival and so it flourished (and at one stage, every grandma in Britain had one).
2) _Very occasionally_, a mutation will give the organism a survival _advantage_ over its relatives. This is _natural selection_ and _evolution_ at work. A good example is a mutation in a bacteria that makes it _resistant to antibiotics_, so the mutant gene _lives on_, in the offspring, creating a _resistant "strain"_ of bacteria.

Don't get your genes in a twist, this stuff's easy...

There are four sections with numbered points for each. _Memorise_ the headings and learn the numbered points, then _cover the page_ and _scribble down_ everything you can remember. I know it makes your head hurt, but every time you try to remember the stuff, the more it sinks in. It'll all be worth it in the end.

Genetic Diseases

Cystic Fibrosis is Caused by a Recessive Gene (Allele)

1) _CYSTIC FIBROSIS_ is a _GENETIC DISEASE_ which affects about _1 in 1600 people_ in the UK.
2) _Both_ parents must have the defective gene for the disorder to be passed on although both may be _carriers_. A carrier is somebody who has the _defective gene_ without actually having the _disorder_.
3) It's a disorder of the _cell membranes_ caused by a _defective gene_. The result of the _defective gene_ is that the body produces a lot of thick sticky mucus in the lungs, which has to be removed by _massage_.
4) _THE BLOCKAGE OF THE AIR PASSAGES_ in the lungs causes a lot of _CHEST INFECTIONS_.
5) _Physiotherapy and antibiotics_ clear them up but slowly the sufferer becomes more and more ill. There's still _no cure_ or effective treatment for this condition.

The _genetics_ behind cystic fibrosis is actually very straightforward. The gene which causes cystic fibrosis is a _recessive gene_, c, carried by about _1 person in 20_. The usual genetic inheritance diagram illustrates what goes on:

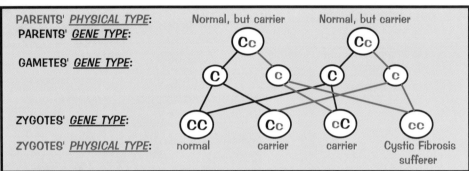

PARENTS' _PHYSICAL TYPE_: Normal, but carrier   Normal, but carrier
PARENTS' _GENE TYPE_: Cc   Cc
GAMETES' _GENE TYPE_: C   c   C   c
ZYGOTES' _GENE TYPE_: CC   Cc   cC   cc
ZYGOTES' _PHYSICAL TYPE_: normal   carrier   carrier   Cystic Fibrosis sufferer

This diagram illustrates _the 1 in 4 chance_ of a child having the disease, _if both parents are carriers_.

Sickle Cell Anaemia — Caused by a Recessive Allele

1) This disease causes the _RED BLOOD CELLS_ to be shaped like _SICKLES_ instead of the normal round shape.
2) They then get _stuck_ in the capillaries which _deprives body cells of oxygen_.
3) Parents may be _carriers_ without actually showing the _symptoms_, but both parents must have the _defective gene_ for the disease to appear in any of their children.
4) Yet even though sufferers _die before they can reproduce_, the occurrence of sickle cell anaemia _doesn't always die out_ as you'd expect it to, especially not in _Africa_.
5) This is because _carriers_ of the recessive allele which causes it _ARE MORE IMMUNE TO MALARIA_. Hence, being a carrier _increases_ their chance of survival in some parts of the world, even though some of their offspring are going to die young from sickle cell anaemia.
6) The genetics are _identical_ to _Cystic Fibrosis_ because both diseases are caused by a _recessive allele_. Hence if _BOTH_ parents are carriers there's a _1 in 4 chance_ each child will develop it:

Normal, but carrier   Normal, but carrier
Ns   Ns
N   s   N   s
NN   Ns   sN   ss
normal   carrier   carrier   Sickle cell sufferer

Huntington's Chorea is caused by a Dominant Allele

1) This disorder of the _nervous system_, results in shaking, erratic body movements and severe mental deterioration.
2) The disorder can be inherited from _one parent_ who has the disorder.
3) The _"carrier"_ parent will of course be a _sufferer_ too since the allele is dominant, but the symptoms do not appear until _after the age of 40_, by which time the allele has been passed on to _children_ and even _grandchildren_. Hence the disease persists.
4) _UNLIKE_ Cystic Fibrosis and Sickle Cell Anaemia, this disease is caused by a _DOMINANT allele_.
5) This results in a _50% CHANCE_ of each child inheriting the disease _IF JUST ONE PARENT_ is a carrier. _THESE ARE SERIOUSLY GRIM ODDS_.

Carrier/sufferer   normal
Hn   nn
H   n   n   n
Hn   Hn   nn   nn
Sufferer   Sufferer   normal   normal

Learn the facts then see what you know...

These diseases are all mentioned in the _syllabus_ and questions on them are _very likely_. You need to _learn_ all this very basic information on all three. _Cover the page_ and _scribble_ it all down.

Menstrual Cycle Hormones

1) The _monthly_ release of an _egg_ from a woman's _ovaries_ and the build up and break down of a protective lining in the _womb_ is called the _menstrual cycle_.

2) _Hormones_ released by the _pituitary gland_ and the _ovaries_ control the different stages of the menstrual cycle.

There are Three Main Hormones involved

1) FSH (Follicle Stimulating Hormone):

1) Produced by the _pituitary gland_.
2) Causes an _egg to develop in one of the ovaries_.
3) Stimulates the _ovaries to produce oestrogen_.

2) OESTROGEN:

1) Produced in the _ovaries_.
2) Causes _pituitary_ to produce _LH_.
3) _Inhibits_ the further release of _FSH_.

3) LH (Luteinising Hormone):

1) Produced by the _pituitary gland_.
2) Stimulates the _release of an egg_ at around the middle of the menstrual cycle.

Oestrogen and _FSH_ can both be used to _artificially_ control fertility (see below).

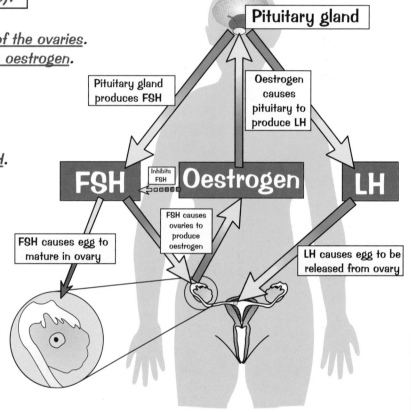

Pituitary gland

Pituitary gland produces FSH

Oestrogen causes pituitary to produce LH

FSH   Inhibits FSH   Oestrogen   LH

FSH causes ovaries to produce oestrogen

FSH causes egg to mature in ovary

LH causes egg to be released from ovary

The control of Fertility

Women who wish to control their fertility can be given extra doses of hormones involved in the menstrual cycle.

Oestrogen is Used to Stop Egg Production in "The PILL"

1) "_THE PILL_", as it's cheerfully known is an oral contraceptive that contains oestrogen.
2) It may seem kind of strange but even though oestrogen stimulates the _release_ of eggs, if oestrogen is taken _every day_ to keep the level of it _permanently high_, it _inhibits_ the production of _FSH_ and _after a while_ egg production _stops_ and stays stopped.

FSH is Used to Stimulate Egg Production in Fertility Treatment

1) A hormone called _FSH_ can be taken by women (who have low levels of FSH) to stimulate _egg production_ in their _ovaries_.
2) In fact _FSH_ (Follicle Stimulating Hormone) stimulates the _ovaries_ to produce _oestrogen_ which in turn stimulates the _release of an egg_.

Well, you gotta be pretty keen to get your head round that lot!

I have to say it's pretty difficult to get a full understanding of how these three hormones all interact with each other to perpetuate the monthly cycle. Basically, as each hormone _increases_, it causes one event or another, and at the _same time_ either _promotes_ or _inhibits_ the production of one of the other hormones. That's how it all keeps going in a cycle, but it's real tricky to understand. So just how keen are you?

Revision Summary for Module Four

Gee, all that business about genes and chromosomes and the like — it's all pretty serious stuff, don't you think? It takes a real effort to get your head round it all. There's too many big fancy words, for one thing. But there you go — life's tough and you've just gotta face up to it.
Use these questions to find out what you know — and what you don't. Then look back and learn the bits you didn't know. Then try the questions again, and again...

1) What are the two types of variation? Describe their relative importance for plants and animals.
2) Name the four factors affecting environmental variation in plants.
3) What causes the small differences between "identical" twins?
4) Draw a set of diagrams showing the relationship between: cell, nucleus, chromosomes, genes, DNA.
5) On P. 14 there are 6 fancy words to do with genetics. List them all — with explanations.
6) Give a definition of mitosis. Draw a set of diagrams showing what happens in mitosis.
7) What is asexual reproduction? Give a proper definition for it. How does it involve mitosis?
8) Where does meiosis take place? What kind of cells does meiosis produce?
9) Draw out the sequence of diagrams showing what happens during meiosis.
10) How many pairs of chromosomes are there in a normal human cell nucleus?
11) What happens to the chromosome numbers during meiosis and then during fertilisation?
12) What is sexual reproduction? Give a proper definition for it.
13) Describe the basic procedure in selective breeding (of cows). Give five other examples.
14) What is meant by selective breeding?
15) Describe the advantages and disadvantages of selective breeding.
16) Give a good account of embryo transplants, and a good account of genetic engineering.
17) Describe the drawbacks and ethical problems concerning the use of genetic engineering.
18) Write down all you know on cloned plants.
19) Describe fully the three ways that fossils can form. Give examples of each type.
20) Describe three places where no decay occurs. Explain why there is no decay.
21) Explain how fossils found in rocks support the theory of evolution. Refer to the horse.
22) Give details about the theory of evolution. Give evidence for the theory.
23) Describe three ways that a species can become extinct.
24) What were Darwin's four observations and two deductions?
25) Describe two examples of how natural selection changes animals.
26) What are X and Y chromosomes to do with? Who has what combination?
27) Copy and complete the genetic inheritance diagram and the checker-board diagram to show how these genes are passed on.

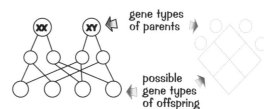

28) Give brief explanations of the following words: a) Allele; b) Homozygous; c) Heterozygous.
29) What are the fancy terms given to the following combinations of genes: a) HH; b) hh; c) Hh.
30) Starting with parental gene types HH and hh, draw a full genetic inheritance diagram to show the eventual gene types and physical types of the F1 and F2 generations (of hamsters).
31) Describe how radiation causes mutations. What else can causes mutations?
32) Name three things that increase the chance of a mutation occurring.
33) List the symptoms and treatment of cystic fibrosis. What causes this disease?
34) Give the cause and symptoms of sickle cell anaemia. Why does it not die out?
35) Explain the grim odds for Huntington's Chorea.
36) Sketch a diagram to show the interaction of the three main hormones in the female menstrual cycle .
37) Give two examples of ways to control the menstrual cycle.

Rates of Reaction

The Rate of a Reaction Depends on Four Things:

1) *TEMPERATURE*
2) *CONCENTRATION* — (or *PRESSURE* for gases)
3) *CATALYST*
4) *SIZE OF PARTICLES* — (or *SURFACE AREA*)

LEARN THEM!

Typical Graphs for Rate of Reaction

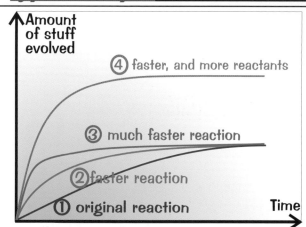

Amount of stuff evolved

④ faster, and more reactants

③ much faster reaction

②faster reaction

① original reaction

Time

1) *Graph 1* represents the original *fairly slow* reaction.
2) *Graphs 2 and 3* represent the reaction taking place *quicker* but with the *same initial amounts*.
3) The *increased rate* could be due to *any* of these:

     a) increase in *temperature*
     b) increase in *concentration* (or pressure)
     c) *catalyst* added
     d) solid reactant crushed up into *smaller bits*.

4) *Graph 4* produces *more product* as well as going *faster*. This can *only* happen if *more reactant(s)* are added at the start.

Reactions can go at all sorts of different rates

1) One of the *slowest* is the *rusting* of iron (it's not slow enough though — what about my little MGB).
2) A *moderate speed* reaction is a *metal* (like magnesium) reacting with *acid* to produce a gentle stream of *bubbles*.
3) A *really fast* reaction is an *explosion*, where it's all over in a *fraction* of a second.

Bang
Bang *Blast*

Three ways to Measure the Speed of a Reaction

The *speed of reaction* can be observed *either* by how quickly the reactants are used up or how quickly the products are forming. It's usually a lot easier to measure *products forming*. There are *three* different ways that the speed of a reaction can be *measured*:

1) Precipitation

This is when the product of the reaction is a *precipitate* which *clouds* the solution. Observe a *marker* through the solution and measure how long it takes for it to *disappear*.

2) Change in mass (usually gas given off)

Any reaction that *produces a gas* can be carried out on a *mass balance* and as the gas is released the mass *disappearing* is easily measured.

CLOUDY

3) The volume of gas given off

This involves the use of a *gas syringe* to measure the volume of gas given off. But that's about all there is to it.

How to get a fast, furious reaction — crack a wee joke...

There's all sorts of bits and bobs of information on this page. To learn it all, you've got to learn to split it up into separate sections and do them one at a time. Practise by *covering the page* and seeing how much you can *scribble down* for each section. *Then try again, and again...*

Collision Theory

Reaction rates are explained perfectly by *Collision Theory*. It's really simple. It just says that the *rate* of a reaction simply depends on how *often* and how *hard* the reacting particles *collide* with each other. The basic idea is that particles have to *collide* in order to *react*, and they have to collide *hard enough* as well.

More Collisions *increase the Rate of Reaction*

All *four* methods of increasing the *rate of reactions* can be *explained* in terms of increasing the *number of collisions* between the reacting particles;

1) TEMPERATURE *increases the number of collisions*

When the *temperature* is *increased* the particles all move *quicker*. If they're moving quicker, they're going to have *more collisions*.

2) CONCENTRATION *(or PRESSURE) increases the number of collisions*

If the solution is made more *concentrated* it means there are more particles of *reactant* knocking about between the water molecules which makes collisions between the *important* particles *more likely*. In a *gas*, increasing the *pressure* means the molecules are *more squashed up* together so there are going to be *more collisions*.

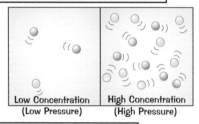

3) SIZE OF SOLID PARTICLES *(or SURFACE AREA) increases Collisions*

If one of the reactants is a *solid* then *breaking it up* into *smaller* pieces will *increase* its surface area. This means the particles around it in the solution will have *more* area to work on so there'll be *more* useful collisions.

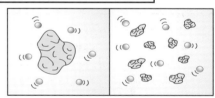

4) CATALYST *increases the number of collisions*

A *catalyst* works by giving the *reacting particles* a *surface* to *stick to* where they can *bump* into each other. This obviously increases the *number of collisions* too.

Surface of catalyst

Faster Collisions *increase the Rate of Reaction*

Higher temperature also increases the *energy* of the collisions, because it makes all the particles move *faster*.

Faster collisions are ONLY caused by increasing the temperature

Reactions *only* happen if the particles collide with *enough* energy. At a *higher temperature* there will be *more particles* colliding with *enough energy* to make the reaction happen. This *initial* energy is known as the *activation energy*, and it's needed to *break* the initial bonds.

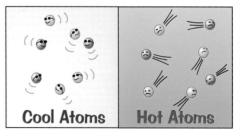

Cool Atoms   Hot Atoms

Collision Theory — I reckon it's always women drivers...

This is quite easy I think. Isn't it all kind of obvious — at least once you've been told it, anyway. The more often particles collide and the harder they hit, the greater the reaction rate. There's a few extra picky details of course (isn't there always!), *but you've only got to LEARN them...*

32

Catalysts

Many reactions can be *speeded up* by adding a *catalyst*.

1) Catalysts Increase the Speed of the Reaction

> A **CATALYST** is a substance which **INCREASES** the speed of a reaction, without being **CHANGED** or **USED UP** in the reaction.

2) Catalysts work best when they have a Big Surface Area

1) Catalysts are usually used as a *powder* or *pellets* or a *fine gauze*.
2) This gives them *maximum surface area* to enable the reacting particles to *meet up* and do the business.

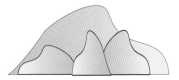

Catalyst Powder

Catalyst Pellets

Catalyst Gauzes

3) Catalysts Help Reduce Costs in Industrial Reactions

1) *Catalysts* increase the rate of many *industrial reactions*, which saves a lot of *money* simply because the plant doesn't need to operate for *as long* to produce the *same amount* of stuff.
2) Alternatively, a catalyst will allow the reaction to work at a *much lower temperature* and that can save a lot of money too. Catalysts are therefore *very important* for *commercial reasons*.
3) Catalysts are used *over and over* again. They may need *cleaning* but they don't get *used up*.
4) Different *reactions* use different *catalysts*.
5) *Transition metals* are common catalysts in many *industrial* reactions. *Know these two*:

a) An Iron Catalyst is used in the Haber Process

$$N_{2(g)} + 3H_{2(g)} \underset{\longleftarrow}{\overset{\text{Iron Catalyst}}{\rightleftharpoons}} 2NH_{3(g)}$$

(See P. 36)

b) A Platinum Catalyst is used in the production of Nitric Acid

$$\text{Ammonia} + \text{Oxygen} \xrightarrow{\text{Platinum Catalyst}} \text{Nitrogen monoxide} + \text{Water}$$

(See P. 37)

Catalysts are like great jokes — you can use them over and over...

Make sure you *learn the definition* in the top box *word for word*. The fact is they can easily ask you: "What is a catalyst?" (2 Marks). This is much easier to answer if you have a "word for word" definition at the ready. If you don't, you're likely to lose half the marks on it. That's a fact.

Enzymes

Enzymes are Biological Catalysts

1) _Living things_ have thousands of different chemical processes going on inside them.
2) The _quicker_ these happen the _better_, and raising the _temperature_ of the body is an important way to _speed them up_.
3) However, there's a _limit_ to how far you can _raise_ the temperature before _cells_ start getting _damaged_, so living things also produce _enzymes_ which act as _catalysts_ to _speed up_ all these chemical reactions without the need for _high temperatures_.

Enzymes are produced by Living Things and are Great

1) Every _different_ biological process has its _own enzyme_ designed especially for it.
2) Enzymes have _two main advantages_ over traditional _non-organic_ catalysts:
   a) They're _not scarce_ like many metal catalysts e.g. platinum.
   b) They _work best_ at low temperatures, which keeps costs down.

Enzymes Like it Warm but Not Too Hot

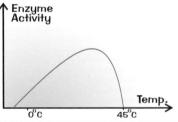

The _chemical reactions_ in _living cells_ are _quite fast_ in conditions that are _warm_ rather than _hot_. This is because the cells use _enzyme_ catalysts, which are _protein molecules_. Enzymes are usually _damaged_ by temperatures above about _45ºC_, and as the graph shows, their activity drops off _sharply_ when the temperature gets _a little too high_.

Yeast in Brewing of Beer and Wine: Fermentation

Yeast cells convert _sugar_ into _carbon dioxide_ and _alcohol_. The main thing is to keep the _temperature_ just right. If it's _too cold_ the enzyme won't work very _quickly_. If it's _too hot_ it will _destroy_ the enzyme.

FERMENTATION is the process of _yeast_ converting _sugar_ into _carbon dioxide_ and _alcohol_.

$$\text{Glucose} \xrightarrow{\text{Zymase}} \text{Carbon dioxide} + \text{Ethanol} \quad (+ \text{ Energy})$$

Yeast in Bread-making: Fermentation again

The reaction in _bread-making_ is _exactly the same_ as that in _brewing_. Yeast cells use the enzyme _zymase_ to break down sugar and this releases carbon dioxide gas as a waste product. The _carbon dioxide gas_ is produced _throughout_ the bread mixture and forms in _bubbles_ everywhere. This makes the bread _rise_ and gives it its familiar texture.

Using Special Bacteria to make Yoghurt

To make yoghurt pasteurised milk is mixed with _specially grown cultures_ of bacteria. The mixture is kept at the _ideal temperature_ for the bacteria and their enzymes to work. For _yoghurt_ this is _pretty warm_ at about _45ºC_. The _yoghurt-making bacteria_ convert _lactose_, (the natural sugar found in milk), into _lactic acid_.

"Enzymes" — sounds like a brand of throat lozenge...

This page is definitely a candidate for the mini-essay method. Two mini-essays in fact. What else is there to say? _Scribble down the facts, then look back and see what you missed_.

Energy Transfer in Reactions

Energy Transfer in Reactions

Whenever chemical reactions occur _energy_ is usually _transferred_ to or from the _surroundings_.

In an Exothermic Reaction, Heat is GIVEN OUT

An _EXOTHERMIC REACTION_ is one which _GIVES OUT ENERGY_ to the surroundings, usually in the form of _HEAT_ and usually shown by a _RISE IN TEMPERATURE_

1) The best example of an _exothermic_ reaction is _burning fuels_. This obviously _gives out a lot of heat_ — it's very exothermic.

2) _Neutralisation reactions_ (acid + alkali) are also exothermic.

3) Addition of water to anhydrous _copper(II) sulphate_ to turn it into blue crystals _produces heat_, so it must be _exothermic_.

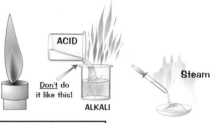

In an Endothermic Reaction, Heat is TAKEN IN

An _ENDOTHERMIC REACTION_ is one which _TAKES IN ENERGY_ from the surroundings, usually in the form of _HEAT_ and usually shown by a _FALL IN TEMPERATURE_

Endothermic reactions are _less common_ and less easy to spot.
So _LEARN_ these three examples, in case they ask for one:

Energy

1) _Photosynthesis_ is endothermic — it _takes in energy_ from the sun.

2) _Dissolving certain salts in water_

    e.g. 1) potassium chloride   2) ammonium nitrate

3) _Thermal decomposition_.

    Heat must be supplied to cause the compound to _decompose_.
    The best example is converting _calcium carbonate_ into _quicklime_ (calcium oxide).

Food

$$CaCO_3 \rightarrow CaO + CO_2$$

A lot of heat energy is needed to make this happen.
In fact the calcium carbonate has to be _heated in a kiln_ and kept at about _800°C_.
It takes almost _30,000kJ_ of heat to make _10kg_ of calcium carbonate decompose.
That's pretty endothermic I'd say, wouldn't you.

Energy Must Always be Supplied to Break bonds... ...and Energy is Always Released When Bonds Form

1) During a chemical reaction, _old bonds_ are _broken_ and _new bonds_ are _formed_.
2) Energy must be _supplied_ to break _existing bonds_ — so bond breaking is an _endothermic_ process.
3) Energy is _released_ when new bonds are _formed_ — so bond formation is an _exothermic_ process.

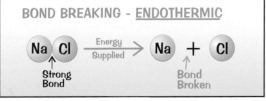

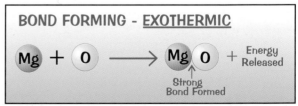

4) In an _exothermic_ reaction, the energy _released_ in bond formation is _greater_ than the energy used in _breaking_ old bonds.
5) In an _endothermic_ reaction, the energy _required_ to break old bonds is _greater_ than the energy _released_ when _new bonds_ are formed.

Energy Transfer in Reactions

Energy Level Diagrams show if it's Exo- or Endo-thermic

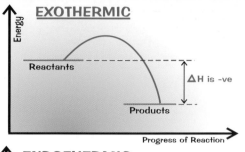

In exothermic reactions ΔH is -ve

1) This shows an _exothermic reaction_ because the products are at a _lower energy_ than the reactants.
2) The difference in _height_ represents the energy _given out_ in the reaction (per mole). ΔH is -ve in this case.
3) The _initial rise_ in the line represents the energy needed to _break_ the old bonds. This is the _activation energy_.

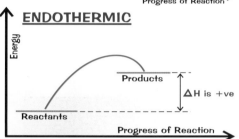

In endothermic reactions ΔH is +ve

1) This shows an _endothermic reaction_ because the products are at a _higher energy_ than the reactants. ΔH _is +ve_.
2) The _difference in height_ represents the _energy taken in_ during the reaction.

The Activation Energy is Lowered by Catalysts

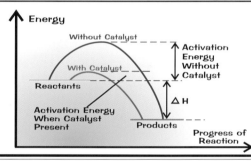

1) The _activation energy_ represents the _minimum energy_ needed by reacting particles for the reaction to occur.
2) A _catalyst_ makes reactions happen _easier_ (and therefore quicker) by _reducing_ the initial energy needed.
3) This is represented by the _lower curve_ on the diagram showing a _lower activation energy_.
4) The _overall energy change_ for the reaction, ΔH, _remains the same_ though.

Bond Energy Calculations — need to be practised!

1) _Every_ chemical bond has a particular _bond energy_ associated with it.
2) This _bond energy_ is always the same no matter what _compound_ the bond occurs in.
3) We can use these _known bond energies_ to calculate the _overall energy change_ for a reaction.
4) You need to _practise_ a few of these, but the basic idea is really very simple.

Example: The Formation of HCl

The bond energies we need: H—H +436kJ/mole; Cl—Cl +242kJ/mole; H—Cl 431kJ/mole.

Using these known bond energies we can _calculate_ the _energy change_ for this reaction:

$$H_2 + Cl_2 \rightarrow 2HCl$$

1) _Breaking_ one mole of H—H and one mole of Cl—Cl bonds _requires_ 436 + 242 = _+678kJ_
2) _Forming two_ moles of H—Cl bonds _releases_ 2×431 = _862kJ_
3) _Overall_ there is more energy _released_ than used: 862 – 678 = _184kJ/mol_ released.
4) Since this is energy _released_, then if we wanted to show ΔH we'd need to put a _–ve_ in front of it to indicate that it's an _exothermic_ reaction, like this: ΔH = -184kJ/mol

Energy transfers and Heat — make sure you take it in...

The stuff about exothermic and endothermic reactions is really quite simple. You've just got to get used to the big words. The bond energy calculations though, now they need quite a bit of practice, as do any kind of calculation questions. You can't just do one or two and think that'll be OK. No way man, you've gotta do loads of them. I'm sure "Teach" will provide you with plenty of practice though. Good old "Teach"!

The Haber Process

This is an *important industrial process*. It produces *ammonia* which is needed for making *fertilisers*.

Nitrogen and Hydrogen are needed to make Ammonia

1) The *nitrogen* is obtained easily from the *AIR*, which is *78% nitrogen* (and 21% oxygen).
2) The *hydrogen* is obtained from *WATER* (steam) and *NATURAL GAS* (methane, CH_4).
   The methane and steam are reacted *together* like this:

$$CH_{4\,(g)} + H_2O_{(g)} \rightarrow CO_{(g)} + 3H_{2\,(g)}$$

3) Hydrogen can also be obtained from *crude oil*.

The Haber Process is a Reversible Reaction:

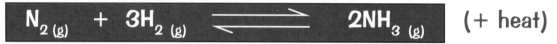

$$N_{2\,(g)} + 3H_{2\,(g)} \rightleftharpoons 2NH_{3\,(g)} \quad (+\text{ heat})$$

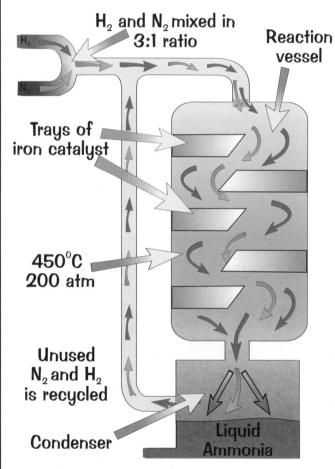

H₂ and N₂ mixed in 3:1 ratio

Reaction vessel

Trays of iron catalyst

450°C 200 atm

Unused N₂ and H₂ is recycled

Condenser

Liquid Ammonia

Industrial conditions:

PRESSURE:	200 atmospheres
TEMPERATURE:	450°C
CATALYST:	Iron

Because the Reaction is Reversible, there's a compromise to be made:

1) *Higher pressures* favour the *forward* reaction, hence the *200 atmospheres* operating pressure.

2) However, it turns out that *lower* temperatures improve the forward reaction. At least it does in terms of the *proportion* of hydrogen and nitrogen converting to ammonia. This is called the *yield*.

3) The trouble is, *lower temperatures* mean a *slower rate of reaction*. (This is different from *yield*.)

4) So the 450°C is a *compromise* between *maximum yield* and *speed of reaction*.

5) The pressure used is also a compromise. Even *higher* pressures would *increase* the yield further, but the plant would be *more expensive to build*. In the end it all comes down to *minimising costs*.

EXTRA NOTES:

1) The hydrogen and nitrogen are mixed together in a *3:1 ratio*.
2) Because the reaction is *reversible*, not all of the nitrogen and hydrogen will *convert* to ammonia.
3) The *ammonia* is formed as a *gas* but as it cools in the condenser it *liquefies* and is *removed*.
4) The N₂ and H₂ which didn't react are *recycled* and passed through again so *none is wasted*.

200 atmospheres? — that could give you a headache..

There are quite a lot of details on this page. They're pretty keen on the Haber process in the Exams so you'd be well advised to learn all this. They could easily ask you on any of these details. Use the same good old method: *Learn it, cover it up, repeat it back to yourself, check, try again...*

Fertiliser from Ammonia

On this page are _two reactions_ involving _ammonia_ that you need to be familiar with. Somehow, I don't think I'd have either of them in my list of "Top Ten Most Riveting Chemistry Topics":

1) Ammonia Can be Oxidised To Form Nitric Acid

There are _two stages_ to this reaction:

a) Ammonia gas reacts with oxygen over a hot platinum catalyst:

$$4NH_{3\,(g)} + 5O_{2\,(g)} \rightarrow 4NO_{(g)} + 6H_2O_{(g)}$$

This first stage is very _exothermic_ and produces it's own heat to _keep it going_.
The nitrogen monoxide must be _cooled_ before the next stage, which happens easily:

b) The nitrogen monoxide reacts with water and oxygen...

$$6NO_{(g)} + 3O_{2\,(g)} + 2H_2O_{(g)} \rightarrow 4HNO_{3\,(g)} + 2NO_{(g)}$$

...to form nitric acid, HNO_3

Gripping stuff. Anyway, the _nitric acid_ produced is _very useful_ for other chemical processes. One such use is to make _ammonium nitrate_ fertiliser...

2) Ammonia can be neutralised with Nitric Acid...

...to make Ammonium Nitrate fertiliser

This is a straightforward and spectacularly unexciting _neutralisation_ reaction between an _alkali_ (ammonia) and an _acid_. The result is of course a _neutral salt_: (prod me if I fall asleep)

$$NH_{3\,(g)} + HNO_{3\,(aq)} \rightarrow NH_4NO_{3\,(aq)}$$
Ammonia + Nitric acid $\rightarrow$ Ammonium nitrate

Ammonium nitrate is an especially good fertiliser because it has _nitrogen_ from _two sources_, the ammonia and the nitric acid. Kind of a _double dose_. Plants need nitrogen to make _proteins_.

Excessive Nitrate Fertiliser causes Eutrophication and Health Problems

1) If _nitrate fertilisers_ wash into _streams_ they set off a cycle of _mega-growth_, _mega-death_ and _mega-decay_. Plants and green algae grow out of control, then start to _die off_ because there's too many of them, then _bacteria_ take over, feeding off the dying plants and using up all the _oxygen_ in the water. Then the fish all die because they can't get enough _oxygen_. Lovely. It's called _eutrophication_ (see the Biology Book for more details). It's all good clean fun.

2) If too many _nitrates_ get into drinking water it can cause _health problems_, especially for young _babies_. Nitrates prevent the _blood_ from carrying _oxygen_ properly and children can _turn blue_ and even _die_.

3) To avoid these problems it's important that artificial nitrate fertilisers are applied _carefully_ by all farmers — they must take care not to apply _too much_, and not if it's _going to rain_ soon.

There's nowt wrong wi' just spreadin' muck on it...

Basically, this page is about how ammonia is turned into ammonium nitrate fertiliser. Alas there are some seriously tedious details which they seem to expect you to learn. Don't ask me why. Anyway, _the more you learn, the more you know_. (He said, wisely and meaninglessly.)

Simple Reversible Reactions

A _reversible reaction_ is one which can go _in both directions_.
In other words the _products_ of the reaction can be _turned back_ into the original _reactants_.
Here are some _examples_ you should know about in case they spring one on you in the Exam.

The Thermal decomposition of Ammonium Chloride

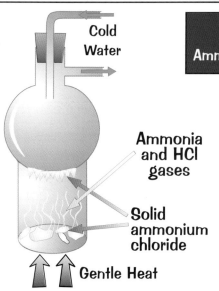

Cold Water

Ammonia and HCl gases

Solid ammonium chloride

Gentle Heat

$$NH_4Cl_{(s)} \rightleftharpoons NH_{3(g)} + HCl_{(g)}$$
Ammonium chloride $\rightleftharpoons$ ammonia + hydrogen chloride

1) When _ammonium chloride_ is _heated_ it splits up into _ammonia gas_ and _HCl gas_.

2) When these gases _cool_ they recombine to form _solid ammonium chloride_.

3) This is a _typical reversible reaction_ because the products _recombine_ to form the original substance _very easily_.

The Thermal decomposition of hydrated copper sulphate

1) Good old dependable _blue copper(II) sulphate_ crystals here again.
2) Here they're displaying their usual trick, but under the guise of a _reversible reaction_.

3) If you _heat them_ it drives the water off and leaves _white anhydrous_ copper(II) sulphate powder.

Water vapour

4) If you then _add_ a couple of drops of _water_ to the _white powder_ you get the _blue crystals_ back again.

The proper name for the _blue crystals_ is _Hydrated Copper(II) sulphate_.   "_Hydrated_" means "_with water_".   When you drive the water off they become a white powder, _Anhydrous copper(II) sulphate_.   "_Anhydrous_" means "_without water_".

Reacting Iodine with Chlorine to get Iodine Trichloride

There's quite a jolly _reversible reaction_ between the mucky brown liquid of _iodine monochloride_ (ICl), and nasty green _chlorine gas_ to form nice clean yellow crystals of _iodine trichloride_ (ICl$_3$).

$$ICl + Cl_2 \rightleftharpoons ICl_3$$

1) Which way the reaction goes depends on the _concentration_ of chlorine gas in the air around.
2) A _lot_ of chlorine will favour formation of the _yellow crystals_.
3) A _lack_ of chlorine will encourage the crystals to _decompose_ back to the horrid brown liquid.

Learn these simple reactions, then see what you know...

These reactions might seem a bit obscure but they're all mentioned in one syllabus or another, so any of them could come up in your Exam. There really isn't much to learn here. _Scribble it._

Reversible Reactions in Equilibrium

Reversible Reactions

A _reversible reaction_ is one where the _products_ can react with each other and _convert back_ to the original chemicals. In other words, _it can go both ways_.

> A _REVERSIBLE REACTION_ IS ONE WHERE THE _PRODUCTS_ OF THE REACTION CAN _THEMSELVES REACT_ TO PRODUCE THE _ORIGINAL REACTANTS_
>
> A + B ⇌ C + D

Reversible Reactions will reach Dynamic Equilibrium

1) If a reversible reaction takes place in a _closed system_ then a state of _equilibrium_ will always be reached.

2) _Equilibrium_ means that the _relative (%) quantities_ of reactants and products will reach a certain _balance_ and stay there. A '_closed system_' just means that none of the reactants or products can _escape_.

3) It is in fact a _DYNAMIC EQUILIBRIUM_, which means that the reactions are still taking place in _both directions_ but the _overall effect is nil_ because the forward and reverse reactions _cancel_ each other out. The reactions are taking place at _exactly the same rate_ in both directions.

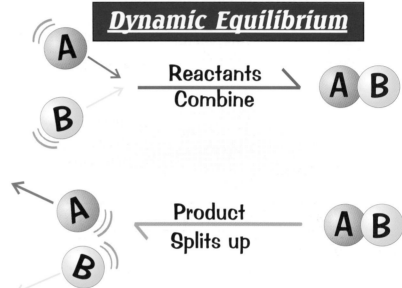

Dynamic Equilibrium

Reactants Combine → A B

Product Splits up ← A B

Changing Temperature and Pressure to get More Product

1) In a reversible reaction the '_position of equilibrium_' (the relative amounts of reactants and products) depends _very strongly_ on the _temperature_ and _pressure_ surrounding the reaction.
2) If we _deliberately alter_ the temperature and pressure we can _move_ the "position of equilibrium" to give _more product_ and _less_ reactants.

Two very simple rules for which way the equilibrium will move

1) All reactions are _exothermic_ in one direction and _endothermic_ in the other.
If we _raise_ the _temperature_, the _endothermic_ reaction will increase to _use up_ the extra heat.
If we _reduce_ the _temperature_ the _exothermic_ reaction will increase to _give out_ more heat.

2) Many reactions have a _greater volume_ on one side, either of _products_ or _reactants_.
If we _raise_ the _pressure_ it will encourage the reaction which produces _less volume_.
If we _lower_ the _pressure_ it will encourage the reaction which produces _more volume_.

Learning/forgetting— the worst reversible of them all...

There's three sections here: the definition of a reversible reaction, the notion of dynamic equilibrium and two equilibrium rules. Make sure you can give a good rendition of all of them.

The Haber Process Again

Other details of the Haber Process are given on P. 36.

The Haber Process _is a controlled_ Reversible Reaction

The Equation is:

$$N_2{}_{(g)} \quad + \quad 3H_2{}_{(g)} \quad \rightleftharpoons \quad 2NH_3{}_{(g)}$$

ΔH is -ve, (see P.35) i.e. the _forward_ reaction is _exothermic_

Higher Pressure _will Favour the_ Forward _Reaction so build it strong..._

1) On the _left side_ of the equation there are _four moles_ of gas (N_2 + $3H_2$), whilst on the _right side_ there are just _two moles_ (of NH_3).

2) So any _increase_ in _pressure_ will favour the _forward reaction_ to produce more _ammonia_. Hence the decision on pressure is _simple_. It's just set _as high as possible_ to give the _best % yield_ without making the plant _too expensive_ to build. 200 to 350 atmospheres are typical pressures used.

Lower Temperature WOULD _favour the forward Reaction BUT..._

The reaction is _exothermic_ in the forward direction which means that _increasing_ the temperature will actually move the equilibrium _the wrong way_, away from ammonia and more towards H_2 and N_2. _But they increase the temperature anyway..._ this is the tricky bit so learn it real good:

LEARN THIS REAL WELL:

1) The _proportion_ of ammonia at equilibrium can only be increased by _lowering_ the temperature.
2) But instead they _raise_ the temperature and accept a _reduced_ proportion (or _yield_) of ammonia.
3) The reason is that the _higher_ temperature gives a much higher _RATE OF REACTION_.
4) It's better to wait just _20 seconds_ for a _10% yield_ than to have to wait _60 seconds_ for a _20% yield_.
5) Remember, the unused hydrogen, H_2, and nitrogen, N_2, are _recycled_ so _nothing is wasted_.

The Iron Catalyst Speeds up the reaction and keeps costs down

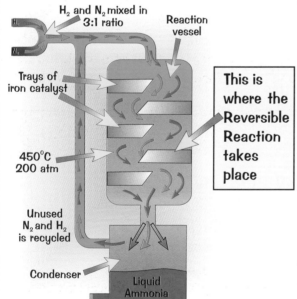

H₂ and N₂ mixed in 3:1 ratio

Reaction vessel

Trays of iron catalyst

This is where the Reversible Reaction takes place

450°C 200 atm

Unused N₂ and H₂ is recycled

Condenser

Liquid Ammonia

1) The _iron catalyst_ makes the reaction go _quicker_ which gets it to the _equilibrium proportions_ more quickly. But remember, the catalyst _doesn't_ affect the _position_ of equilibrium (i.e. the % yield).

2) _Without the catalyst_ the temperature would have to be _raised even further_ to get a _quick enough_ reaction and that would _reduce the % yield_ even further. So the catalyst is very important.

3) _Removing product_ would be an effective way to improve yield because the reaction keeps _chasing equilibrium_ while the product keeps _disappearing_. Eventually _the whole lot_ is converted.

4) This _can't be done_ in the Haber Process because the ammonia can't be removed until _afterwards_ when the mixture is _cooled_ to _condense out_ the ammonia.

Learning the Haber process — it's all ebb and flow...

If they're going to use any reversible reaction for an Exam question, it'll probably be this one. The trickiest bit is that the temperature is raised not for a better equilibrium, but for speed. Try the mini-essay method to _scribble down all you know_ about equilibrium and the Haber process.

Relative Formula Mass

The biggest trouble with _RELATIVE ATOMIC MASS_ and _RELATIVE FORMULA MASS_ is that they _sound_ so bloodcurdling. _"With big scary names like that they must be really, really complicated"_ I hear you cry. Nope, wrong. They're dead easy. Take a few deep breaths, and just enjoy, as the mists slowly clear...

Relative Atomic Mass, A_r — _easy peasy_

1) This is just a way of saying how _heavy_ different atoms are _compared to each other_.
2) The _relative atomic mass_ A_r is nothing more than the _mass number_ of the element.
3) On the periodic table, the elements all have _two_ numbers. The smaller one is the atomic number (how many protons it has).
   But the _bigger one_ is the _mass number_ (how many protons and neutrons it has) which, kind of obviously, is also the _Relative atomic mass_. Easy peasy, I'd say.

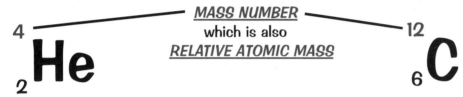

Helium has $A_r = 4$. Carbon has $A_r = 12$. (So carbon atoms are _3 times heavier_ than helium atoms)

Relative Formula Mass, M_r — _also easy peasy_

If you have a compound like $MgCl_2$ then it has a _RELATIVE FORMULA MASS_, M_r, which is just all the relative atomic masses _added together_.
For $MgCl_2$ it would be:

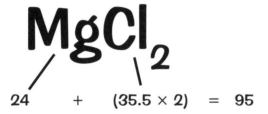

$$24 \quad + \quad (35.5 \times 2) \quad = \quad 95$$

> So the M_r for $MgCl_2$ is simply <u>95</u>

You can easily get the A_r for any element from the _Periodic Table_ (see inside front cover), but in a lot of questions they give you them anyway. I tell you what, since it's nearly Christmas I'll run through another example for you:

<u>Question:</u> _Find the relative formula mass for calcium carbonate, $CaCO_3$ using the given data:_
A_r for Ca = 40 A_r for C = 12 A_r for O = 16

ANSWER:

CaCO₃

$$40 \quad + \quad 12 \quad + \quad (16 \times 3) = 100$$

> So the Relative Formula Mass for $CaCO_3$ is <u>100</u>

And that's all it is. A big fancy name like _Relative Formula Mass_ and all it means is _"add up all the mass numbers"_. What a swizz, eh? You'd have thought it'd be something a bit juicier than that, wouldn't you. Still, that's life — it's all a big disappointment in the end. Sigh.

Phew, Chemistry — _scary stuff sometimes, innit..._

When you know it, _cover the page_ and _scribble down_ the important details. D'ya miss any?
1) Use the periodic table to find the relative atomic mass of these elements: Cu, K, Kr, Fe, Cl
2) Also find the relative formula mass of these compounds: NaOH, Fe_2O_3, C_6H_{14}, $Mg(NO_3)_2$

Two Formula Mass Calculations

Although Relative Atomic Mass and Relative Formula Mass are *easy enough*, it can get just a tadge *trickier* when you start getting into other calculations which use them. It depends on how good your maths is basically, because it's all to do with ratios and percentages.

Calculating % Mass *of an Element in a Compound*

This is actually dead easy — so long as you've learnt this formula:

$$\text{PERCENTAGE MASS OF AN ELEMENT IN A COMPOUND} = \frac{A_r \times \text{No. of atoms (of that element)}}{M_r \quad \text{(of whole compound)}} \times 100$$

If you don't learn the formula then you'd better be pretty smart — or you'll struggle.

EXAMPLE: Find the percentage mass of sodium in sodium carbonate, Na_2CO_3
ANSWER:

A_r of sodium = 23, A_r of carbon = 12, A_r of oxygen = 16
M_r of Na_2CO_3 = $(2 \times 23) + 12 + (3 \times 16) = 106$

Now use the formula: $Percentage\ mass = \dfrac{A_r \times n}{M_r} \times 100 = \dfrac{23 \times 2}{106} \times 100 = 43.4\%$

And there you have it. Sodium represents *43.4%* of the mass of sodium carbonate.

Finding The Empirical Formula *(from Masses or Percentages)*

This also sounds a lot worse than it really is. Try this for an easy peasy *stepwise method*:

1) *LIST ALL THE ELEMENTS* in the compound (there's usually only two or three!).
2) *Underneath them*, write their *EXPERIMENTAL MASSES OR PERCENTAGES*.
3) *DIVIDE* each mass or percentage *BY THE A_r* for that particular element.
4) Turn the numbers you get into *A NICE SIMPLE RATIO*
   by multiplying and/or dividing them by well-chosen numbers.
5) Get the ratio in its *SIMPLEST FORM*, and that tells you the formula of the compound.

EXAMPLE: Find the empirical formula of the iron oxide produced when 44.8g of iron react with 19.2g of oxygen. (A_r for iron = 56, A_r for oxygen =16)
METHOD:

	Fe	O
1) List the two elements:	Fe	O
2) Write in the *experimental masses*:	44.8	19.2
3) Divide by the A_r for each element:	$44.8/56 = 0.8$	$19.2/16 = 1.2$
4) Multiply by 10...	8	12
...then divide by 4:	2	3

5) So the *simplest formula* is 2 atoms of Fe to 3 atoms of O, i.e. Fe_2O_3. And that's it done.

> You need to realise (for the Exam) that this *EMPIRICAL METHOD* (i.e. based on *experiment*) is the *only way* of finding out the formula of a compound. Rust is iron oxide, sure, but is it FeO, or Fe_2O_3? Only an experiment to determine the empirical formula will tell you for certain.

Old Dmitri Mendeleev did this sort of stuff in his sleep — the old rogue...

Make sure you *learn the formula* at the top and the five rules in the red box. Then try these:
1) Find the percentage mass of oxygen in these: a) Fe_2O_3 b) H_2O c) $CaCO_3$ d) H_2SO_4
2) Find the empirical formula when 2.4g of carbon reacts with 0.8g of hydrogen.

Calculating Masses in Reactions

These can be kinda scary too, but chill out, little white-faced one — just relax and enjoy.

The Three Important Steps — not to be missed...

(Miss one out and it'll all go horribly wrong, believe me)

1) *WRITE OUT* the balanced *EQUATION*
2) *Work out M_r* — just for the *TWO BITS YOU WANT*
3) Apply the rule: *DIVIDE TO GET ONE, THEN MULTIPLY TO GET ALL*
(But you have to apply this first to the substance they give information about, and *then* the other one!)

EXAMPLE: *What mass of magnesium oxide is produced when 60g of magnesium is burned in air?*

ANSWER:

1) Write out the BALANCED EQUATION:

$$2Mg + O_2 \rightarrow 2MgO$$

2) Work out the RELATIVE FORMULA MASSES:

(don't do the oxygen — we don't need it)

$$2 \times 24 \rightarrow 2 \times (24+16)$$
$$48 \rightarrow 80$$

3) Apply the rule: *DIVIDE TO GET ONE, THEN MULTIPLY TO GET ALL*

The two numbers, 48 and 80, tell us that *48g of Mg react to give 80g of MgO*.
Here's the 0 bit. You've now got to be able to write this down:

48g of Mg ......reacts to give.....80g of MgO

1g of Mg ......reacts to give.....

60g of Mg .....reacts to give......

THE BIG CLUE is that in the question they've said we want to burn "*60g of magnesium*"
i.e. they've told us how much *magnesium* to have, and that's how you know to write down the
LEFT HAND SIDE of it first, because:

We'll first need to ÷ by 48 to get 1g of Mg
and then need to × by 60 to get 60g of Mg.

THEN you can work out the numbers on the other side (shown in orange below) by realising
that you must *divide BOTH sides by 48* and then *multiply BOTH sides by 60*. It's tricky.

÷48 48g of Mg .... 80g of MgO ÷48
     1g of Mg .... 1.67g of MgO
×60 60g of Mg .... 100g of MgO ×60

You should realise that *in practise* 100% yield may not be obtained in some reactions, so the amount of product might be *slightly less than calculated.*

This finally tells us that *60g of magnesium will produce 100g of magnesium oxide.*
If the question had said "Find how much magnesium gives 500g of magnesium oxide.", you'd fill in the MgO side first instead, *because that's the one you'd have the information about*. Got it? Good-O!

Reaction Mass Calculations? — no worries, matey...

Learn the three rules in the red box and practise the example till you can do it fluently.
1) Find the mass of calcium which gives 30g of calcium oxide (CaO), when burnt in air.

Calculating Volumes

These are OK as long as you *LEARN* the formula in the *RED BOX* and know how to use it.

1) *Calculating the Volume When you know the Masses*

For this type of question there are *TWO STAGES*:

1) *Find the reacting mass*, exactly like in the examples on the last page.
2) Then *convert the mass into a volume* using this formula:

$$\frac{\text{VOL. OF GAS (in cm}^3)}{24,000} = \frac{\text{MASS OF GAS}}{M_r \text{ of gas}}$$

This formula comes from the well known(!) fact that:

A MASS OF M_r IN GRAMS, of any gas, will always occupy *24 LITRES*
(at room temperature and pressure) — and it's the same for *ANY GAS*.

I reckon it's easier to learn and use the formula, but it's certainly worth knowing that fact too.

EXAMPLE: Find the volume of carbon dioxide produced (at room T and P) when 2.7g of carbon is
completely burned in oxygen. (A_r of carbon = 12, A_r of oxygen = 16)

ANSWER:

1) Balanced equation: $C \quad + \quad O_2 \quad \rightarrow \quad CO_2$

2) Fill in M_r for each: $\div 12$ (12   32   44   ) $\div 12$

3) Divide for one, times for all: 1 .... $\boxed{3.6666667}$

                 $\times 2.7$ (2.7 .... $\boxed{9.8999999}$) $\times 2.7$

                                            = 9.9

4) So 2.7g of C gives 9.9g of CO_2.
Now the new bit:

5) *USING THE ABOVE FORMULA:*

$$\frac{\text{Volume}}{24,000} = \frac{\text{MASS}}{M_r} \qquad \text{Volume} = \frac{\text{MASS}}{M_r} \times 24,000$$

so Volume = (MASS/M_r) × 24,000 = (9.9/44) × 24000 = $\boxed{5400.}$

                                   = <u>5400cm³</u> or <u>5.40 litres</u>

2) *Calculating the Mass when you're given the Volume*

For this type of question the *TWO STAGES* are in the *reverse order*:

1) First *find the mass from the volume* using the same formula as before:

$$\frac{\text{VOL. OF GAS (in cm}^3)}{24,000} = \frac{\text{MASS OF GAS}}{M_r \text{ of gas}}$$

2) Then *find the reacting mass*, exactly like in the examples on the last page.

EXAMPLE: Find the mass of 6.2 litres of oxygen gas. (A_r of oxygen = 16)

ANSWER: Using the above formula: $\dfrac{6,200}{24,000} = \dfrac{\text{Mass of Gas}}{32}$

                                                    (Look out, 32, because it's O_2)

Hence,   Mass of Gas = (6,200/24,000) × 32 = $\boxed{8.2666667}$ = <u>8.27g</u>

The question would likely go on to ask what mass of CO_2 would be produced if this much oxygen reacted with
carbon. In that case you would now just apply the same old method from the previous page (as used above).

Calculating Volumes — it's just a gas...

Make sure you *learn the formula* in the red box at the top and that you know how to use it.
1) Find the volume of 2.5g of methane gas, CH_4. (at room T & P).
2) Find the mass of oxide (MgO) produced when magnesium is burned with 1.7 litres of oxygen.

Electrolysis Calculations

The important bit here is to get the balanced half equations, because they determine *THE RELATIVE AMOUNTS* of the two substances produced at the two electrodes. After that it's all the same as before, working out masses using M_r values, and volumes using the "$M_r(g)$ = 24 litres" rule.

The Three Steps for Electrolysis Calculations

1) Write down the *TWO BALANCED HALF EQUATIONS*
   (i.e. match the number of electrons)
2) Write down the *BALANCED FORMULAE* for the
   two products obtained from the two electrodes.
3) *WRITE IN THE M_r VALUES* underneath each
   and carry on as for previous calculations.

EXAMPLE: In the electrolysis of sodium chloride, sodium is deposited at the cathode and chlorine gas is released at the anode. If 2.5g of sodium are collected at the cathode, find the volume of chlorine released.

ANSWER:

1) Balanced *half equations*:

$$2Na^+ + 2e^- \rightarrow 2Na$$
$$2Cl^- - 2e^- \rightarrow Cl_2$$

(2×23 because it's 2Na not just Na)

2) Balanced formulae of *products*:
   (as obtained from the balanced half equations)

(2×35.5 because it's Cl_2 not just Cl)

3) Write in M_r values:
   ...and carry on as usual

	2Na	Cl_2	
÷46	46	71	÷46
	1 .... 1.5434782		
×2.5	2.5 .... 3.8586956		×2.5

= **3.86**

So 2.5g of sodium will yield 3.86g of chlorine gas. Now we need this as a volume, so we use the good old '*mass to volume converting formula*':

$$Volume = \frac{MASS}{24,000} \quad \Rightarrow \quad Volume = \frac{MASS \times 24,000}{M_r} = \frac{3.86 \times 24,000}{71} = \boxed{1304.3478}$$

$$= \underline{1304 cm^3}$$

And there it is, done in a flash. Just the same old stuff every time isn't it — balanced formulae, fill in M_r values, "divide and times" on both sides, and then use the "24,000 rule" to find the volume. Trivial.

Calculation of A_r from % abundances of Isotopes

Some elements, like chlorine, have A_r values which are not whole numbers. This is because there are *TWO STABLE ISOTOPES* of chlorine, ^{35}Cl and ^{37}Cl, and the mixture of the two gives an average A_r of 35.5. There is a simple formula for working out the overall A_r from the percentage abundances of two different isotopes:

$$Overall\ A_r = [(A_1 \times \%_{(1)}) + (A_2 \times \%_{(2)})] \div 100$$

FOR EXAMPLE if chlorine consists of 76% ^{35}Cl and 24% ^{37}Cl, then the overall value for A_r is:
Overall $A_r = [(35 \times 76) + (37 \times 24)] \div 100 = 35.48 = \underline{35.5}$ to 1 d.p.

Electrolysis — keep your hair on, it's not that bad...

With electrolysis calculations the main tricky bit is getting the balanced half equations right and then using the balanced symbol amounts for both products (e.g. 2Na and Cl_2).

1) In the electrolysis of aluminium oxide, Al_2O_3 if 23kg of aluminium is deposited at the cathode, what volume of oxygen will be liberated at the anode (when it's cooled down to room T and P anyway!)

Revision Summary for Module Seven

This module isn't too bad really. I suppose some of the stuff on Rates of Reaction and Relative Formula Mass gets a bit chewy in places, but the rest is all a bit of a breeze really, isn't it? Anyway, here's some more of those nice easy questions which you enjoy so much. Remember, if you can't answer one, look at the appropriate page and learn it. Then go back and try them again. Your hope is that one day you'll be able to glide effortlessly through all of them — it's a nice trick if you can do it.

1) What are the four factors which the rate of a reaction depends on?
2) What are the three different ways of measuring the speed of a reaction? Describe each method as fully as possible, using a diagram.
3) Explain how each of the four factors that increase the rate of a reaction increase the *number of collisions* between particles.
4) What is the other aspect of collision theory which determines the rate of reaction?
5) What is the definition of a catalyst?
6) Why is it best to maximise the surface area of a catalyst? How is this done?
7) Give the word-equation for fermentation. Which organism and which enzyme are involved?
8) Explain what happens in brewing and bread-making. What is the difference between them?
9) What are endothermic and exothermic reactions? Give three examples of each type.
10) Draw energy level diagrams for these two types of reaction.
11) How do bond breaking and bond forming relate to these diagrams?
12) What are bond energies and what can you calculate from them?
13) What is the Haber process? What are the raw materials for it and how are they obtained?
14) Draw a full diagram for the Haber process and explain the temperature and pressure used.
15) Give full details of how ammonia is turned into nitric acid, including equations.
16) Give two problems resulting from the use of nitrate fertilisers.
17) What is a reversible reaction? Describe three simple reversible reactions involving solids.
18) Explain what is meant by dynamic equilibrium in a reversible reaction.
19) How does changing the temperature and pressure of a reaction alter the equilibrium?
20) How does this influence the choice of pressure for the Haber Process?
21) What determines the choice of operating temperature for the Haber process?
22) Find A_r or M_r for these (use the periodic table inside the front cover):
   a) Ca   b) Ag   c) CO_2 d) $MgCO_3$ e) Na_2CO_3 f) ZnO   g) butane   h) sodium chloride
23) What is the formula for calculating the percentage mass of an element in a compound?
   a) Calculate the percentage mass of oxygen in magnesium oxide, MgO
   b) Calculate the percentage mass of carbon in   i) $CaCO_3$ ii) CO_2 iii) Methane
   c) Calculate the percentage mass of metal in these oxides: i) Na_2O ii) Fe_2O_3 iii) Al_2O_3
24) What is meant by an empirical formula?
25) Work these out (using the periodic table):
   a) Find the EF for the iron oxide formed when 45.1g of iron reacts with 19.3g of oxygen.
   b) Find the EF for the compound formed when 227g of calcium reacts with 216g of fluorine.
26) Write down the three steps of the method for calculating reacting masses.
   a) What mass of magnesium oxide is produced when 112.1g of magnesium burns in air?
   b) What mass of sodium is needed to produce 108.2g of sodium oxide?
27) Write down the formula for calculating the volume of a known mass of gas (at room T & P).
   a) What is the volume of 56.0g of nitrogen at room T & P?
   b) What mass of carbon dioxide is produced when 4.7 litres of oxygen reacts with carbon?
28) a) In the electrolysis of NaCl, find the mass of Cl_2 released if 3.4g of sodium are collected.
   b) In the electrolysis of copper(II) chloride, what volume of chlorine gas would be produced for every 100g of copper obtained?

Solids, Liquids and Gases

These are known as the *three states of matter*. Make sure you know everything there is to know.

Solids have Strong Forces of Attraction

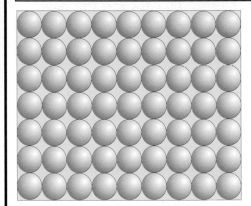

1) There are *strong forces* of *attraction* between molecules.
2) The molecules are held in *fixed positions* in a very regular lattice arrangement.
3) They *don't* move from their positions, so all solids keep a definite *shape* and *volume*, and don't flow like liquids.
4) They *vibrate* about their positions. The *hotter* the solid becomes, the *more* they *vibrate*. This causes solids to *expand* slightly when heated.
5) Solids *can't be compressed* because the molecules are already packed *very* closely together.
6) Solids are generally *very* dense.

Liquids have Moderate Forces of Attraction

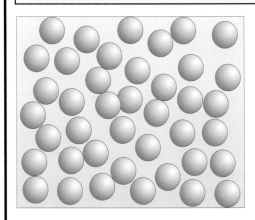

1) There is *some* force of *attraction* between the molecules.
2) The molecules are *free* to move past each other, but they do tend to *stick* together.
3) Liquids *don't* keep a *definite shape* and will flow to fill the bottom of a container. But they do keep the *same* volume.
4) The molecules are *constantly* moving in *random* motion. The *hotter* the liquid becomes, the *faster* they move. This causes liquids to *expand* slightly when heated.
5) Liquids *can't* be compressed because the molecules are already packed *closely* together.
6) Liquids are *quite dense*, but not as dense as solids.

Gases have No Forces of Attraction

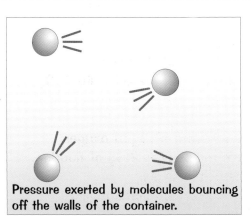

Pressure exerted by molecules bouncing off the walls of the container.

1) There is *no* force of *attraction* between the molecules.
2) The molecules are free to move. They travel in *straight lines* and only interact with each other when they *collide*.
3) Gases *don't* keep a *definite* shape or volume and will always *expand* to fill any container. Gases exert a *pressure* on the walls of the container.
4) The molecules are *constantly* moving in *random* motion. The *hotter* the gas becomes, the *faster* they move. When *heated*, a gas will either *expand* or its *pressure* will *increase*.
5) *Gases* can be *compressed* easily because there's a lot of *free space* between the molecules.
6) Gases all have very low *densities*.

Don't get yourself in a state about this lot, just learn it...

This is pretty basic stuff, but people still lose marks in the Exam because they don't make sure to learn all the little details really thoroughly. And there's only one way to do that: *COVER THE PAGE UP AND SCRIBBLE IT ALL DOWN FROM MEMORY*. That soon shows what you really know — and that's what you've got to do for every page. Do it now for this one, *AND KEEP TRYING UNTIL YOU CAN*.

Changes of State

CHANGES OF STATE always involve *HEAT ENERGY* going either *IN* or *OUT*.

Melting — the rigid lattice breaks down

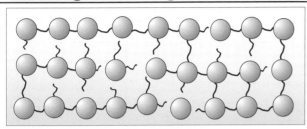

1) When a *SOLID* is *heated*, the heat energy goes to the *molecules*.
2) It makes them vibrate *more and more*.
3) Eventually the *strong forces* between the molecules (that hold them in the rigid lattice) are *overcome*, and the molecules start to move around. The solid has now *MELTED*.

Evaporation — the fastest molecules escape

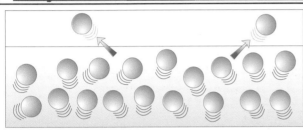

1) When a *LIQUID* is *heated*, the heat energy goes to the *molecules*, which makes them *move faster*.
2) Some molecules move faster than others.
3) Fast-moving molecules at the *surface* will *overcome* the forces of *attraction* from the other molecules and *escape*. This is *EVAPORATION*.

Boiling — all molecules are fast enough to escape

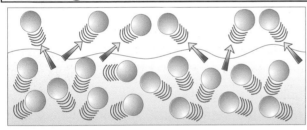

1) When the liquid gets *hot enough*, virtually *all* the molecules have enough *speed and energy* to overcome the forces and *escape* each other.
2) At this point big *bubbles* of *gas* form inside the liquid as the molecules break away from each other. This is *BOILING*.

Heating and Cooling Graphs Have Important Flat Spots

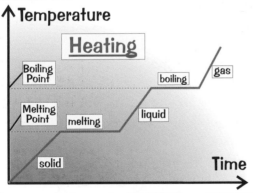

1) When a substance is *MELTING* or *BOILING*, all the *heat energy* supplied is used for *breaking bonds* rather than raising the temperature, hence the flat spots in the heating graph.
2) When a liquid is *cooled*, the graph for temperature will show a flat spot at the *freezing* point.
3) As the molecules *fuse* into a solid, *HEAT IS GIVEN OUT* as the bonds form, so the temperature *won't* go down until *all* the substance has turned to *solid*.

Revision — don't get all steamed up about it...

There are five diagrams and a total of 11 numbered points on this page. They wouldn't be there if you didn't need to learn them. *So learn them.* Then cover the page and scribble them all down. You have to realise this is the only way to really learn stuff properly. *And learn it you must.*

Brownian Motion and Diffusion

1) Brownian motion is the _jerky movement_ of _smoke_ particles, as seen through a microscope.
2) It's caused by _air_ molecules _bumping_ into the _smoke_ particles and knocking them about.
3) The smoke particles _reflect the light_ shone onto them — they're seen as _bright specks_.
4) Brownian motion can also be seen in _pollen grains in water_, looked at through a microscope.

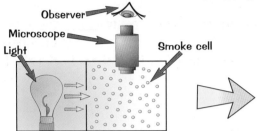

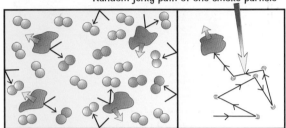

Random jerky path of one smoke particle

Three Gripping Diffusion Experiments

1) _DIFFUSION_ is when two gases or liquids merge together to form a mixture.
2) It happens because the _molecules_ in liquids and gases are in _constant rapid random motion_.
   Make sure you can explain what's happening in these three demonstrations.

1) _Purple Potassium Manganate(VII) in water_

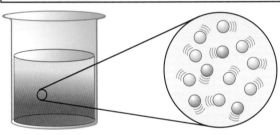

1) As it _dissolves_ into the water, the molecules of the purple potassium manganate(VII) gradually _diffuse_ through the _liquid_.
2) The constant _rapid random motion_ of all the molecules causes the purple colour to eventually spread _evenly_ through the whole liquid.

2) _Good old Boring Brown Bromine in Air and in Vacuum_

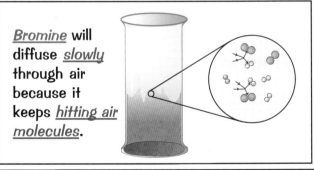

Bromine will diffuse _slowly_ through air because it keeps _hitting air molecules_.

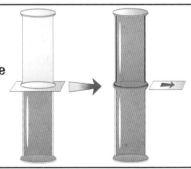

But in a _vacuum_ bromine spreads _instantly_ because there are _no_ air molecules to get in the way.

3) _Diffusion of Hydrochloric Acid and Ammonia_

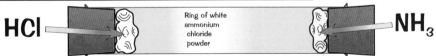

HCl   Ring of white ammonium chloride powder   NH₃

1) The cotton wool pads are soaked in _ammonia_ and _HCl_ and shoved into the ends of the tube.
2) The two liquids _evaporate_ and _diffuse_ through the air.
3) When they meet they form _ammonium chloride_, a white solid, visible inside the tube.
4) The _ring of white powder_ forms _nearer_ to the HCl end because the _ammonia_ travels _faster_.
5) This is because ammonia molecules are _lighter_, and lighter molecules always travel _faster_.

Diffusion — it's just a riot, don't you think...

When you think you know the whole page, _cover it up_ and scribble down all the diagrams together with the numbered points for each one. Turn back and _learn_ the bits you forgot. Then try again.

Atoms

The structure of atoms is real simple. I mean, gee, there's nothing to them. Just learn and enjoy.

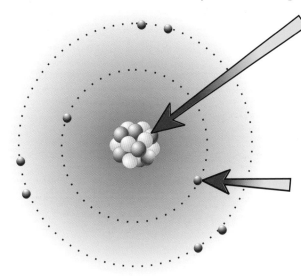

Atoms are *real tiny*, don't forget. They're *too small to see*, even with a microscope.

The Nucleus

1) It's in the *middle* of the atom.
2) It contains *protons* and *neutrons*.
3) It has a *positive charge* because of the protons.
4) Almost the *whole* mass of the atom is *concentrated* in the nucleus.
5) But size-wise it's *tiny* compared to the rest of the atom.

The Electrons

1) Move *around* the nucleus.
2) They're *negatively charged*.
3) They're *tiny*, but they cover *a lot of space*.
4) The *volume* their orbits occupy determines how big the atom is.
5) They have virtually *no* mass.
6) They occupy *shells* around the nucleus.
7) These shells explain *the whole of Chemistry*.

Number of Protons Equals Number of Electrons

1) Neutral atoms have *no charge* overall.
2) The *charge* on the electrons is the *same* size as the charge on the *protons* but *opposite*.
3) This means the *number* of *protons* always equals the *number* of *electrons* in a *neutral atom*.
4) If some electrons are *added or removed*, the atom becomes *charged* and is then an *ION*.
5) The number of neutrons isn't fixed but is usually just a bit *higher* than the number of protons.

Know Your Particles

PROTONS are *HEAVY* and *POSITIVELY CHARGED*
NEUTRONS are *HEAVY* and *NEUTRAL*
ELECTRONS are *Tiny* and *NEGATIVELY CHARGED*

PARTICLE	MASS	CHARGE
Proton	1	+1
Neutron	1	0
Electron	$\frac{1}{2000}$	-1

THE MASS NUMBER

— Total of Protons and Neutrons

THE PROTON NUMBER

— Number of Protons

$$^{23}_{11}\text{Na}$$

POINTS TO NOTE

1) The *proton number* (or *atomic number*) tells you how many *protons* there are (oddly enough).
2) This *also* tells you how many *electrons* there are.
3) The *proton number* is what distinguishes one particular element from another.
4) To get the number of *neutrons* — just *subtract* the *proton number* from the *mass number*.
5) The *mass* number is always the *biggest* number. It tells you the relative mass of the atom.
6) The *mass* number is always roughly *double* the *proton* number.
7) Which means there's about the *same* number of protons as neutrons in any nucleus.

Atoms, Elements and Compounds

Isotopes are the _same_ except for an extra _neutron_ or two

ISOTOPES ARE: different atomic forms of the same element, which have the SAME number of PROTONS but a DIFFERENT number of NEUTRONS.

1) The upshot is: isotopes must have the _same_ proton number but _different_ mass numbers.
2) _If_ they had _different_ proton numbers, they'd be _different_ elements altogether.
3) A very popular pair of isotopes are _carbon-12_ and _carbon-14_.

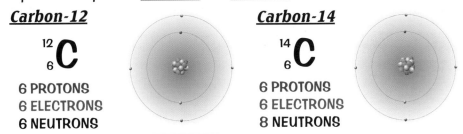

Carbon-12

$^{12}_{6}\text{C}$

6 PROTONS
6 ELECTRONS
6 NEUTRONS

Carbon-14

$^{14}_{6}\text{C}$

6 PROTONS
6 ELECTRONS
8 NEUTRONS

Elements and Compounds

You'd better be sure you know the _subtle difference_ between these.

Elements consist of one type of atom only

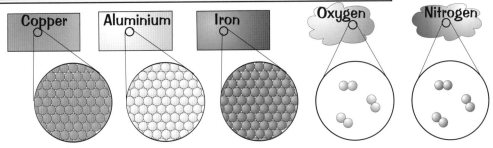

Copper   Aluminium   Iron   Oxygen   Nitrogen

Compounds are chemically bonded

1) Carbon dioxide is a _compound_ formed from a _chemical reaction_ between carbon and oxygen.
2) It's _very difficult_ to _separate_ the two original elements out again.
3) The _properties_ of a compound are _totally different_ from the properties of the _original elements_.
4) If iron and sulphur react to form _iron sulphide_, the compound formed is a _grey solid lump_, and doesn't behave _anything like_ either iron or sulphur.

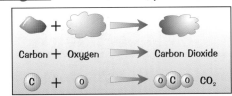

Carbon + Oxygen $\longrightarrow$ Carbon Dioxide

C + O $\longrightarrow$ O C O CO_2

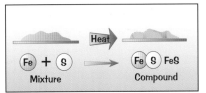

Fe + S $\xrightarrow{\text{Heat}}$ Fe S FeS
Mixture   Compound

5) Don't confuse compounds with mixtures.
   A _mixture_ consists of two or more elements or compounds _not chemically combined together_. The chemical properties of _each substance_ in the mixture are _unchanged_.
6) _Air_ is a _mixture_ of gases. The oxygen, nitrogen, argon and carbon dioxide _can all be separated out quite easily_.

Basic Atom facts — they don't take up much space...

This stuff on atoms should be permanently engraved in the minds of everyone.
I don't understand how people can get through the day without knowing this stuff, really I don't.
LEARN IT NOW, and watch as the Universe unfolds and reveals its timeless mysteries to you...

Electron Shells

The fact that electrons occupy "shells" around the nucleus is what causes the whole of chemistry. Remember that, and watch how it applies to each bit of it. It's ace.

Electron Shell Rules:

1) Electrons always occupy _SHELLS_ (sometimes called _ENERGY LEVELS_).
2) The _LOWEST_ energy levels are _ALWAYS FILLED FIRST_.
3) Only _a certain number_ of electrons are allowed in each shell:
   1st shell: 2   _2nd Shell:_ 8   _3rd Shell:_ 8
4) Atoms are much _HAPPIER_ when they have _FULL electron shells_.
5) In most atoms the _OUTER SHELL_ is _NOT FULL_ and this makes the atom want to _REACT_.

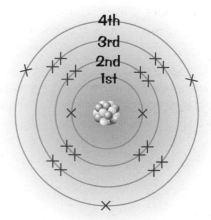

4th shell still filling

Working out Electron Configurations

You need to know the _electron configurations_ for the first _20_ elements. But they're not hard to work out. For a quick example, take Nitrogen. _Follow the steps..._

1) The periodic table (see below) tells us Nitrogen has _seven_ protons... so it must have _seven_ electrons.
2) Follow the '_Electron Shell Rules_' above. The _first_ shell can only take 2 electrons and the _second_ shell can take a _maximum_ of 8 electrons.

3) So the electron configuration for Nitrogen _must_ be _2,5_. Easy peasy.
4) Now _you_ try it for Argon.

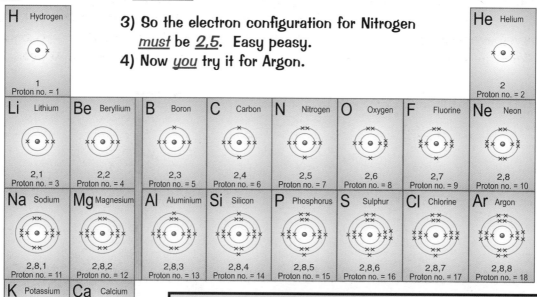

Answer... To calculate the electron configuration of argon, _follow the rules_. It's got 18 protons, so it _must_ have 18 electrons. The first shell must have _2_ electrons, the second shell must have _8_, and so the third shell must have _8_ as well. It's as easy as _2,8,8_.

Electrons rule...

There's some _really important stuff_ on this page and you _really do_ need to _learn all of it_. Once you have, it'll make all of the rest of the stuff in this book an awful lot _easier_. Practise calculating _electron configurations_ and drawing _electron shell_ diagrams.

Electron Shells and Ions

Simple Ions — Groups 1 & 2 and 6 & 7

1) Remember, atoms that have _lost_ or _gained_ an electron (or electrons) are _ions_.
2) The elements that most readily form ions are those in Groups 1, 2, 6, and 7.
3) _Group 1 and 2 elements_ are _metals_ and they _lose_ electrons to form _+ve ions_ or _cations_.
4) _Group 6 and 7 elements_ are _non-metals_. They _gain_ electrons to form _–ve ions_ or _anions_.
5) Make sure you know these easy ones:

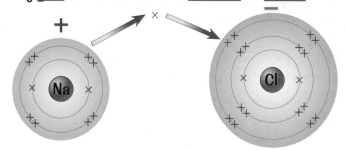

CATIONS		ANIONS	
Gr I	Gr II	Gr VI	Gr VII
Li^+	Be^{2+}	O^{2-}	F^-
Na^+	Mg^{2+}	Cl^-	
K^+	Ca^{2+}		

6) When any of the above elements _react together_, they form _ionic bonds_.
7) Only elements at _opposite sides_ of the periodic table will form ionic bonds, e.g. Na and Cl, where one of them becomes a _CATION_ (+ve) and one becomes an _ANION_ (–ve).

> Remember, the + and – charges we talk about, e.g. Na^+ for sodium, just tell you what type of ion the atom WILL FORM in a chemical reaction. In sodium _metal_ there are _only neutral sodium atoms, Na_. The Na^+ ions _will only appear_ if the sodium metal _reacts_ with something like water or chlorine.

Electronic structure of some simple ions

A useful way of representing ions is by specifying the _ion's name_, followed by its _electron configuration_ and the _charge_ on the ion. For example, the electronic structure of the sodium ion Na^+ can be represented by $[2,8]^+$. That's the electron configuration followed by the charge on the ion. Simple enough. A few _ions_ and the _ionic compounds_ they form are shown below.

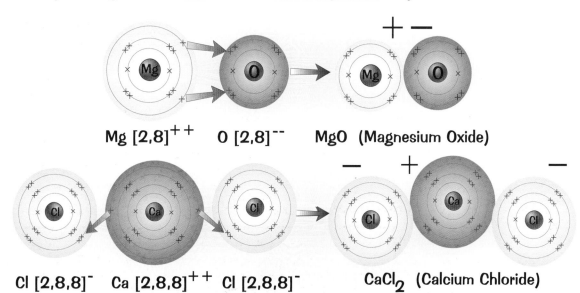

Mg $[2,8]^{++}$ O $[2,8]^{--}$ MgO (Magnesium Oxide)

Cl $[2,8,8]^-$ Ca $[2,8,8]^{++}$ Cl $[2,8,8]^-$ $CaCl_2$ (Calcium Chloride)

Simple ions — looks simple enough to me...

Yet again, more stuff you've _got_ to know. _LEARN_ which atoms form 1+, 1-, 2+ and 2- ions, and why. You need to know how to represent ions _both_ in [x,y] notation _and_ by diagrams. When you think you've got it, _cover the page_ and start scribbling to see what you really know. Then look back, _learn the bits you missed_, and _try again_. And again.

Ionic Bonding

Ionic Bonding — Swapping Electrons

In *IONIC BONDING*, atoms *lose or gain electrons* to form *charged particles* (ions) which are then *strongly attracted* to one another, (the attraction of opposite charges, + and –).

A shell with just one electron is well keen to get rid...

All the atoms over at the *left hand side* of the periodic table, such as *sodium, potassium, calcium* etc. have just *one or two electrons* in their outer shell. And basically they're *pretty keen to get shot of them*, because then they'll only have *full shells* left, which is how they *like* it. So given half a chance they do get rid, and that leaves the atom as an *ION* instead. Now ions aren't the kind of things that sit around quietly watching the world go by. They tend to *leap* at the first passing ion with an *opposite charge* and stick to it like glue.

A nearly full shell is well keen to get that extra electron...

On the *other side* of the periodic table, the elements in *Group Six* and *Group Seven*, such as *oxygen* and *chlorine* have outer shells which are *nearly full*. They're obviously pretty keen to *gain* that *extra one or two electrons* to fill the shell up. When they do of course they become *IONS*, you know, not the kind of things to sit around, and before you know it, *POP*, they've latched onto the atom (ion) that gave up the electron a moment earlier. The reaction of sodium and chlorine is a *classic case*:

The *sodium* atom *gives up* its *outer electron* and becomes an Na$^+$ ion.

The *chlorine* atom *picks up* the *spare electron* and becomes a Cl$^-$ ion.

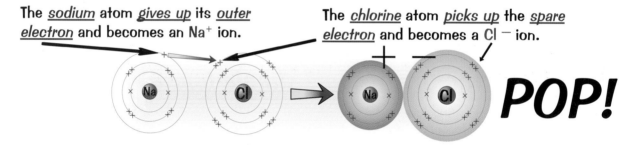

POP!

Giant Ionic Structures don't melt easily, but when they do...

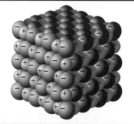

1) *Ionic bonds* always produce *giant ionic structures*.
2) The ions form a *closely packed* regular lattice arrangement.
3) There are *very strong* chemical bonds between *all* the ions.
4) A single crystal of salt is *one giant ionic lattice*, which is why salt crystals tend to be cuboid in shape.

1) They have *High melting points and boiling points*

due to the *very strong* chemical bonds between *all the ions* in the giant structure.

2) They *Dissolve to form solutions that conduct electricity*

When dissolved the ions *separate* and are all *free to move* in the solution, so obviously they'll *carry electric current*.

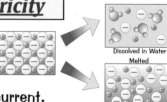

Dissolved in Water

Melted

3) They *Conduct electricity when molten*

When it *melts*, the ions are *free to move* and they'll carry electric current.

Full Shells — it's the name of the game, pal...

Make sure you know exactly *how* and *why* ionic bonds are formed. There's quite a lot of words on this page but only to hammer home *three basic points*: 1) Ionic bonds involve *swapping* electrons   2) Some atoms like to *lose* them, some like to *gain* them   3) Ionic bonds lead to the formation of giant ionic structures. Learn *all* the features of giant ionic structures.

Covalent Bonding

Covalent Bonds — Sharing Electrons

1) Sometimes atoms prefer to make _COVALENT BONDS_ by _sharing_ electrons with other atoms.
2) This way _both_ atoms feel that they have a _full outer shell_, and that makes them happy.
3) Each _covalent bond_ provides one _extra_ shared electron for each atom.
4) Each atom involved has to make _enough_ covalent bonds to _fill up_ its outer shell.
5) _LEARN_ these _FIVE IMPORTANT EXAMPLES_:

1) _Hydrogen Gas, H_$_2$

Hydrogen atoms have just one electron. They _only need one more_ to complete the first shell...

_Or_

H—H

...so they often form _single covalent bonds_ to achieve this.

2) _Hydrogen Chloride HCl_

This is very similar to H$_2$. Again, both atoms _only need one more electron_ to complete their outer shells.

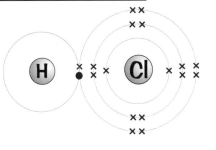

_or_   H—Cl

3) _Ammonia, NH_$_3$

Nitrogen has _five_ outer electrons...

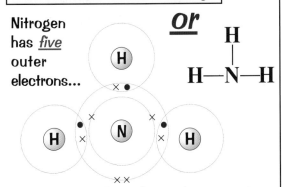

_Or_

H
|
H—N—H

...so it needs to form _three covalent bonds_ to make up the extra _three_ electrons needed.

4) _Methane, CH_$_4$

Carbon has _four outer electrons_, which is a _half full_ shell.

_Or_

```
    H
    |
H — C — H
    |
    H
```

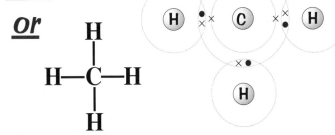

To become a 4+ or a 4− ion is hard work so it forms _four covalent bonds_ to make up its outer shell.

5) _Water, H_$_2$_O_

_Or_

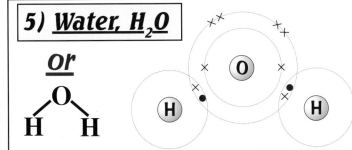

The _oxygen_ atom has _six_ outer electrons. Sometimes it forms _ionic_ bonds by _taking_ two electrons to complete the outer shell. However it will also cheerfully form _covalent bonds_ and _SHARE_ two electrons instead, as in the case of _water molecules_, where it _shares_ electrons with the H atoms.

Full Shells — you just can't beat them...

LEARN the four numbered points about covalent bonds and the five examples.
Then turn over and scribble it all down again. Make sure you can draw all five molecules and explain exactly why they form the bonds that they do. _All from memory of course._

Covalent Substances: Two Kinds

Substances formed from _covalent bonds_ can either be _simple molecules_ or _giant structures_.

Simple Molecular Substances

1) The atoms form _very strong_ covalent bonds to form _small_ molecules of several atoms.
2) By contrast, the forces of attraction _between_ these molecules are _very weak_.
3) The result of these feeble _inter-molecular forces_ is that the _melting-_ and _boiling-points_ are _very low_, because the molecules are _easily parted_ from each other.
4) Most molecular substances are _gases or liquids_ at room temperature.
5) Molecular substances _don't conduct electricity_, simply because there are _no ions_.
6) They _don't dissolve in water_, usually.
7) You can usually tell a molecular substance just from its _physical state_, which is always kinda '_mushy_' — i.e. _liquid_ or _gas_ or an _easily-melted solid_.

Very weak inter-molecular forces

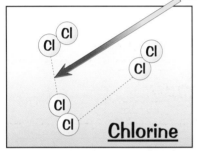

Chlorine

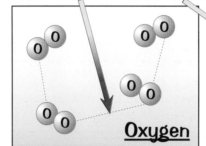

Oxygen

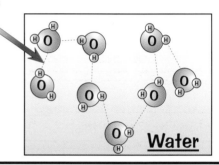

Water

Giant Covalent Structures

1) These are similar to giant ionic structures except that there are _no charged ions_.
2) _All_ the atoms are _bonded_ to _each other_ by _strong_ covalent bonds.
3) They have _very high_ melting and boiling points.
4) They _don't conduct electricity_ — not even when _molten_.
5) They're usually _insoluble_ in water.
6) The _main examples_ are _Diamond_ and _Graphite_ which are both made only from _carbon atoms_.

Diamond

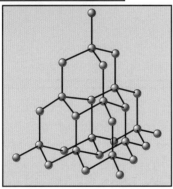

Each carbon atom forms _four_ _covalent bonds_ in a _very rigid_ giant covalent structure.

Graphite

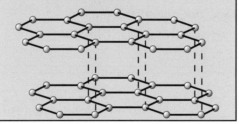

Each carbon atom only forms _three_ _covalent bonds_, creating _layers_ which are free to _slide over each other_, and leaving _free electrons_, so graphite is the only _non-metal_ which _conducts electricity_.

Silicon Dioxide

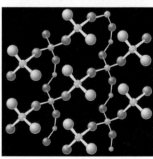

Sometimes called _silica_, this is what _sand_ is made of.
Each grain of sand is _one giant structure_ of silicon and oxygen.

Come on — pull yourself together...

There are two types of covalently bonded substances — and they're totally different. Make sure you know all the details about them and the examples too. _This is real basic stuff_ — just easy marks to be won... or lost. _Cover the page_ and see how many marks you're gonna _WIN_.

Metallic and Plastic structures

Metal Properties are all due to the Sea of Free Electrons

1) _Metals_ also consist of a _giant structure_.
2) _Metallic bonds_ involve the all-important '_free electrons_', which produce _all_ the properties of metals. These free electrons come from the _outer shell_ of _every_ metal atom in the structure.
3) These electrons are _free to move_ and so metals conduct _heat and electricity_.
4) These electrons also _hold_ the atoms together in a regular structure.
5) They also allow the atoms to _slide_ over each other causing metals to be _malleable_.

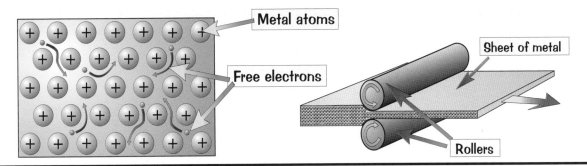

Metal atoms

Free electrons

Sheet of metal

Rollers

Thermosoftening and Thermosetting Plastics

The diagrams show the different types of bonding in these two _different types_ of plastic.

In a _THERMOSOFTENING PLASTIC_, the long chains have no '_cross links_' so, as the plastic is heated, the long chains _loosen_ their weak grip on their neighbours and the plastic goes _soft_. This will happen _every time_ the plastic is heated. As soon as it _cools_ the long chains _attract_ each other again, the weak bonds _reform_, and the plastic becomes more _rigid_ again.

In a _THERMOSETTING PLASTIC_, there are no cross-bonds _initially_, and the first time the plastic is heated it goes soft. However, covalent bond _crosslinks_ then _form_ between the long-chain polymers, and when the plastic sets, it sets for good and _will not_ soften again. The new crosslinks make the plastic much _stronger_.

Thermosoftening Plastic

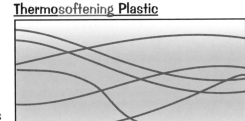

Thermosetting Plastic

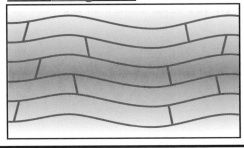

Identifying the bonding in a substance by its properties

If you've learnt the properties of the _six types_ of substance properly, together with their _names_ of course, then you should be able to easily _identify_ most substances just by the way they _behave_ as either: _ionic_, _giant-covalent_, _molecular_, _metallic_, _thermosoftening_ or _thermosetting_. The way they're likely to test you in the Exam is by describing the _physical properties_ of a substance and asking you to decide _which type of bonding_ it has and therefore what type of material it is. If you know your onions you'll have no trouble at all. If not, you're gonna struggle.

Bonding — where would we all be without it...

A good approach here is the _mini-essay method_, where you just write down everything you can about each section, and then look back to see what you missed. This is much better than trying to remember the numbered points in the right order. _Try it for all six types of bonding_.

A History of The Periodic Table

The early Chemists were keen to try and find _patterns_ in the elements.
They had _two_ obvious ways to categorise elements:

1) Their _physical_ and _chemical_ properties   **2) Their _Relative Atomic Mass_**

Remember, they had _no idea_ of _atomic structure_ or of protons or electrons, so there was _no_ such thing as _proton number_ to them. (It was only in the 20th Century after protons and electrons were discovered, that it was realised the elements should be arranged in order of _proton number_.)

Newlands' Octaves Were The First Good Effort

A chap called _Newlands_ had the first good stab at it in _1863_. He noticed that every _eighth_ element had similar properties and so he listed some of the known elements in rows of seven:

Li	Be	B	C	N	O	F
Na	Mg	Al	Si	P	S	Cl

These sets of eight were called _Newlands' Octaves_, but unfortunately the pattern _broke down_ on the _third row_ with many _transition metals_ like Fe and Cu and Zn messing it up completely.

Dmitri Mendeleev Left Gaps and Predicted New Elements

1) In _1869_, _Dmitri Mendeleev_ in Russia, armed with about 50 known elements, arranged them into his Table of Elements with various _gaps_.
2) Mendeleev ordered the elements in order of _atomic mass_ (like Newlands did).
3) But Mendeleev found he had to leave _gaps_ in order to keep elements with _similar properties_ in the same _vertical groups_ — and he was prepared to leave some very _big_ gaps in the first two rows before the transition metals come in on the _third_ row.
4) The _gaps_ were really clever because they _predicted_ the properties of _undiscovered_ elements.

The Modern Periodic Table is Ace

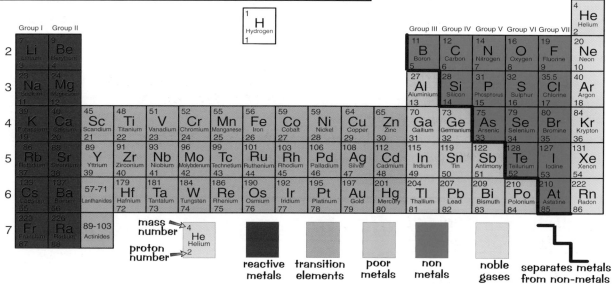

1) The modern Periodic Table shows the elements in order of _proton number_.
2) The Periodic Table is laid out so that elements with _similar properties_ form in _columns_.
3) These _vertical columns_ are called _Groups_ and Roman Numerals are often used for them.
4) For example the _Group II_ elements are Be, Mg, Ca, Sr, Ba and Ra.
    They're all _metals_ which form 2+ ions and they have many other similar properties.
5) The _rows_ are called _periods_. Each new period represents another _full shell_ of electrons.
6) The elements in each _Group_ all have the same number of _electrons_ in their _outer shell_.
7) That's why they have _similar properties_. And that's why we arrange them in this way.

Electron Arrangements

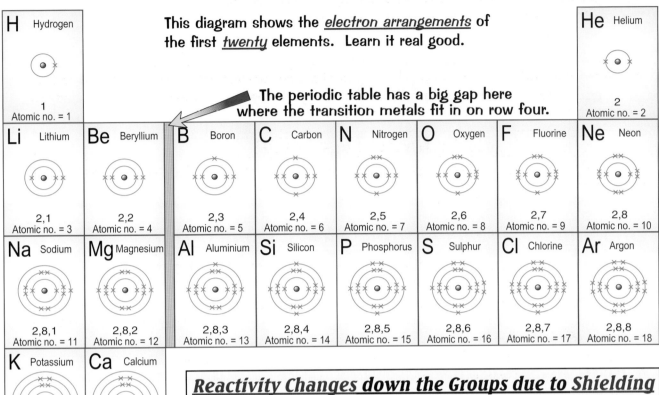

This diagram shows the *electron arrangements* of the first *twenty* elements. Learn it real good.

The periodic table has a big gap here where the transition metals fit in on row four.

H Hydrogen — 1, Atomic no. = 1		He Helium — 2, Atomic no. = 2

Li Lithium 2,1 Atomic no. = 3 · Be Beryllium 2,2 Atomic no. = 4 · B Boron 2,3 Atomic no. = 5 · C Carbon 2,4 Atomic no. = 6 · N Nitrogen 2,5 Atomic no. = 7 · O Oxygen 2,6 Atomic no. = 8 · F Fluorine 2,7 Atomic no. = 9 · Ne Neon 2,8 Atomic no. = 10

Na Sodium 2,8,1 Atomic no. = 11 · Mg Magnesium 2,8,2 Atomic no. = 12 · Al Aluminium 2,8,3 Atomic no. = 13 · Si Silicon 2,8,4 Atomic no. = 14 · P Phosphorus 2,8,5 Atomic no. = 15 · S Sulphur 2,8,6 Atomic no. = 16 · Cl Chlorine 2,8,7 Atomic no. = 17 · Ar Argon 2,8,8 Atomic no. = 18

K Potassium 2,8,8,1 Atomic no. = 19 · Ca Calcium 2,8,8,2 Atomic no. = 20

Reactivity Changes *down the Groups due to Shielding*

1) As Atoms get *bigger*, they have more *full shells* of electrons.
2) As you go down any Group, each *new row* has *one more* full shell.
3) The number of *outer* electrons is the *same* for each element in a Group.
4) However the outer shell of electrons is *increasingly far* from the nucleus.
5) You have to learn to say that the inner shells provide *'SHIELDING'*.
6) This means that the *outer shell* electrons get *shielded* from the *attraction* of the *+ve nucleus*. The upshot of all this is:

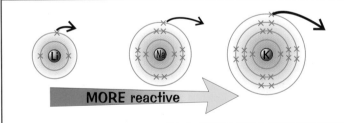

MORE reactive

As metal atoms get bigger, the outer electron is more easily lost.

This makes **METALS MORE REACTIVE** as you go **DOWN** Group I and Group II

As non-metal atoms get bigger, the extra electrons are harder to gain.

This makes **NON-METALS LESS REACTIVE** as you go **DOWN** Group VI and Group VII

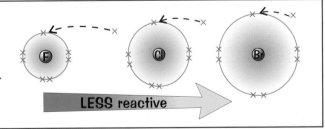

LESS reactive

I Can't see what all the fuss is — it all seems quite elementary...

Make sure you learn the whole periodic table including every name, symbol and number. No only kidding! Just *learn* the numbered points and *scribble* them down, *mini-essay style*. Really, you should be able to draw any of the atoms at the top of the page. Obviously you don't learn every atom separately - you learn the pattern.

MODULE EIGHT — STRUCTURES AND BONDING   NEAB MODULAR SYLLABUS

Transition Metals

These are the transition metals

| | | Sc | Ti | V | Cr | Mn | Fe | Co | Ni | Cu | Zn | | | | | | |

Here they are, right in the middle.

Chromium, Manganese, Iron, Nickel, Copper, Zinc

You need to know the ones shown in red fairly well. If they wanted to be mean in the Exam *(if!)* they could cheerfully mention one of the others like scandium or cobalt or titanium or vanadium. Don't let it hassle you. They'll just be testing how well you can *"apply scientific knowledge to new information"*. In other words, just assume these "new" transition metals follow all the properties you've already learnt for the others. That's all it is, but it can really worry some folk.

Transition Metals all have high melting point and high density

They're *typical* metals. They have the properties you would expect of a proper metal:
1) *Good conductors* of heat and electricity.
2) Very *dense*, *strong* and *shiny*.
3) Iron melts at 1500°C, copper melts at 1100°C and zinc melts at 400°C.

Transition Metals and their compounds all make good catalysts

1) *Iron* is the catalyst used in the *Haber process* for making *ammonia*.
2) *Manganese (IV) oxide* is a good catalyst for the decomposition of *hydrogen peroxide*.
3) *Nickel* is useful for turning *oils into fats* for making margarine.

The compounds are very colourful

1) The compounds are colourful due to the *transition metal ion* which they contain. e.g. Potassium chromate (VI) is *yellow*.
   Potassium manganate(VII) is *purple*.
   Copper (II) sulphate is *blue*.
2) The colour of people's *hair* and also the colours in *gemstones* like *blue sapphires* and *green emeralds* are all due to *transition metals*.

Transition metals produce many useful alloys

1) The transition metals can be easily *mixed* (when molten) to produce a *new* metal with different properties to the original metals. The new metal is called an *alloy*.
2) For example, the transition metals *zinc* and *copper* make the alloy *brass* for trumpets and tubas.

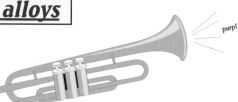

Lots of pretty colours — that's what we like to see...

There's quite a few things to learn about transition metals. First try to remember the three headings. Then learn the details that go under each one. *Keep trying to scribble it all down.*

Group O — The Noble Gases

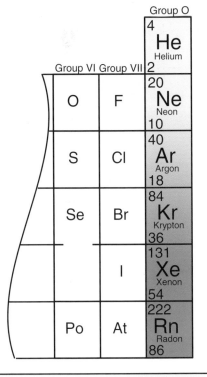

Group VI	Group VII	Group O	
		4 **He** Helium 2	
O	F	20 **Ne** Neon 10	
S	Cl	40 **Ar** Argon 18	
Se	Br	84 **Kr** Krypton 36	
	I	131 **Xe** Xenon 54	
Po	At	222 **Rn** Radon 86	

As you go down the Group:

1) The density *increases*
because the atomic mass increases.

2) The boiling point *increases*
Helium boils at –269°C (that's cold!)
Xenon boils at –108°C (that's still cold)

They all have *full outer shells*
— *That's why they're so inert*

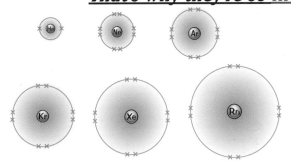

HELIUM, NEON AND ARGON ARE NOBLE GASES
There's also *Krypton*, *Xenon* and *Radon*, which may get asked.
They're also sometimes called the *Inert* gases. Inert means "doesn't react".

THEY'RE ALL COLOURLESS, MONATOMIC GASES
Most gases are made up of *molecules*, but these *only exist* as
individual atoms, because they *won't form bonds* with anything.

THE NOBLE GASES *DON'T REACT AT ALL*
Helium, Neon and Argon don't form *any kind of chemical bonds* with anything.
They *always* exist as separate atoms. They won't even join up in pairs.

HELIUM *IS USED IN AIRSHIPS AND PARTY BALLOONS*
Helium is ideal: it has very *low density* and *won't
set on fire*, (like hydrogen does!)

NEON *IS USED IN ELECTRICAL DISCHARGE TUBES*
When a current is passed through neon it gives out a bright light.

ARGON *IS USED IN FILAMENT LAMPS (LIGHT BULBS)*
It provides an *inert atmosphere* which stops the very hot
filament from *burning away*.

ALL THREE ARE USED IN LASERS TOO
There's the famous little red *Helium-Neon* laser
and the more powerful *Argon laser*.

They don't react — that's Noble De-use to us Chemists...
Well they don't react so there's obviously not much to learn about these. Nevertheless, there's
likely to be several questions on them so *make sure you learn everything on this page*.

Group 1 — The Alkali Metals

Learn These Trends:

As you go *DOWN* Group I,
the Alkali Metals become:

1) *Bigger atoms*
...because there's one extra full shell of electrons for each row you go down.

2) *More Reactive*
...because the outer electron is more easily lost, because it's further from the nucleus.

3) *Higher density*
because the atoms have more mass.

4) *Even Softer to cut*

5) *Lower melting point*

6) *Lower boiling point*

Group I	Group II
7 **Li** Lithium 3	Be
23 **Na** Sodium 11	Mg
39 **K** Potassium 19	Ca
85.5 **Rb** Rubidium 37	Sr
133 **Cs** Caesium 55	Ba
223 **Fr** Francium 87	Ra

These *Group II* metals are quite similar to Group I, except that they have two electrons in the outer shell and form 2+ ions. They are less reactive.

---

1) *The Alkali metals are very Reactive*
They have to be *stored in oil* and handled with *forceps* (they burn the skin).

2) *They are: Lithium, Sodium, Potassium and a couple more*
Know those three names real well. They may also mention Rubidium and Caesium.

3) *The Alkali Metals all have ONE outer electron*
This makes them very *reactive* and gives them all similar properties.

4) *The Alkali Metals all form 1⁺ ions*

They are *keen to lose* their one outer electron to form a *1^+ ion*:

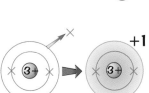

5) *The Alkali metals always form Ionic Compounds*
They are so keen to lose the outer electron there's *no way* they'd consider *sharing*, so covalent bonding is *out of the question*.

6) *The Alkali metals are soft — they cut with a knife*
Lithium is the hardest, but still easy to cut with a scalpel.
They're *shiny* when freshly cut, but *soon go dull* as they react with the air.

7) *The Alkali metals melt and boil easily (for metals)*
Lithium melts at 180°C, Caesium at 29°C. Lithium boils at 1330°C, Caesium at 670°C.

8) *The Alkali metals have low density (they float)*
Lithium, Sodium and Potassium are all *less dense than water*. The others *"float"* anyway, on H_2.

Learn about Alkali Metals — or get your fingers burnt...

Phew, now we're getting into the seriously dreary facts section. This takes a bit of learning this stuff does, especially those trends in behaviour as you go down the group. *Enjoy.*

Reactions of the Alkali Metals

Periodic Table

Reaction with Cold Water produces *Hydrogen Gas*

1) When *lithium*, *sodium* or *potassium* are put in *water*, they react very *vigorously*.
2) They *move* around the surface, *fizzing* furiously.
3) They produce *hydrogen*. Potassium gets hot enough to *ignite* it.
   A lighted splint will *indicate* hydrogen by producing
   the notorious "*squeaky pop*" as the H_2 ignites.
4) Sodium and potassium *melt* in the heat of the reaction.
5) They form a *hydroxide* in solution, i.e. *aqueous OH⁻ ions*.

$$2Na_{(s)} + 2H_2O_{(l)} \rightarrow 2NaOH_{(aq)} + H_{2\,(g)}$$
$$2K_{(s)} + 2H_2O_{(l)} \rightarrow 2KOH_{(aq)} + H_{2\,(g)}$$

The solution becomes *alkaline*, which changes the colour of the pH indicator to *purple*.

Reaction with *Chlorine* etc. to produce *Neutral Salts*

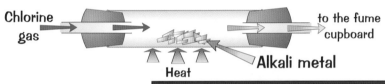

Chlorine gas → → → to the fume cupboard

Heat ↑↑↑ Alkali metal

Lithium, *sodium* and *potassium* all react *very vigorously* with *chlorine* when *heated*. They produce chloride salts.

Learn these easy equations:

$$2Na_{(s)} + Cl_{2\,(g)} \rightarrow 2NaCl_{(s)} \quad \text{(sodium chloride)}$$
$$2K_{(s)} + Cl_{2\,(g)} \rightarrow 2KCl_{(s)} \quad \text{(potassium chloride)}$$

Fluorine, *bromine* and *iodine* produce similar salts. They all cheerfully *dissolve* in water.

Alkali Metals burn in Air to produce Oxides

They all *burn in air* with *pretty coloured flames*:

Lithium: $4Li_{(s)} + O_{2\,(g)} \rightarrow 2Li_2O_{(s)}$ (lithium oxide)   *Bright red* flame

Sodium: $4Na_{(s)} + O_{2\,(g)} \rightarrow 2Na_2O_{(s)}$ (sodium oxide)   *Bright orange* flame

Potassium: $4K_{(s)} + O_{2\,(g)} \rightarrow 2K_2O_{(s)}$ (potassium oxide)   *Bright lilac* flame

Alkali Metal Oxides and Hydroxides are Alkaline

This means that they'll react with *acids* to form *neutral salts*, like this:

$$NaOH + HCl \rightarrow H_2O + NaCl \text{ (salt)}$$
$$Na_2O + 2HCl \rightarrow H_2O + 2NaCl \text{ (salt)}$$

All Alkali Compounds *look like 'Salt'* and *Dissolve with Glee*

1) All alkali metal compounds are *ionic*, so they form *crystals* which *dissolve* easily.
2) They're all very *stable* because the alkali metals are so *reactive*.
3) Because they always form *ionic* compounds with *giant ionic lattices*
   the compounds *all* look pretty much like the regular '*salt*' you put in your chip butties.

The Notorious Squeaky Pop? — weren't they a Rock Band...

This stuff's pretty grisly isn't it. Still, if you keep covering the page and repeating bits back to yourself, or scribbling bits down, then little by little *it does go in*. Little by little. *Nicely*.

Group VII — The Halogens

Learn These Trends:

As you go _DOWN_ Group VII, the _HALOGENS_ have the following properties:

1) _Less Reactive_

2) _Higher melting point_

3) _Higher boiling point_

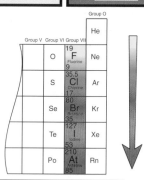

1) The Halogens are all non-metals with coloured vapours

Fluorine is a very reactive, poisonous _yellow gas._

Chlorine is a fairly reactive poisonous _dense green gas._

Bromine is a dense, poisonous, _red-brown volatile liquid._

Iodine is a _dark grey_ crystalline _solid_ or a _purple vapour._

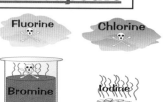

2) They all form molecules which are pairs of atoms:

 F_2 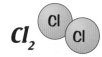 Cl_2 Br Br Br_2 I I I_2

3) The Halogens do both ionic and covalent bonding

The Halogens all form _ions with a 1⁻ charge_: F^- Cl^- Br^- I^- as in Na^+Cl^- or $Fe^{3+}Br^-_3$

They form _covalent bonds_ with _themselves_ and in various _molecular compounds_ like these:

Carbon tetrachloride:

(CCl_4)

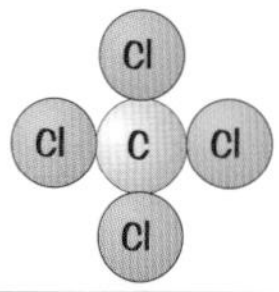

Hydrogen chloride:

(HCl)

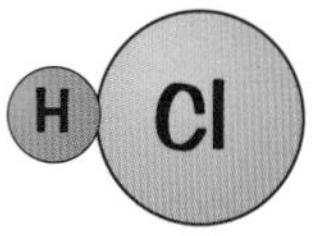

4) The Halogens react with metals to form salts

They react with most metals including _iron_ and _aluminium_, to form _salts_ (or '_metal halides_').

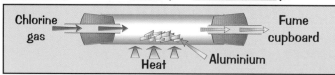
Chlorine gas → Fume cupboard
Heat   Aluminium

$$2Al_{(s)} + 3Cl_{2(g)} \rightarrow 2AlCl_{3(s)}$$
(Aluminium chloride)

$$2Fe_{(s)} + 3Br_{2(g)} \rightarrow 2FeBr_{3(s)}$$
(Iron(III) bromide)

5) More reactive Halogens will displace less reactive ones

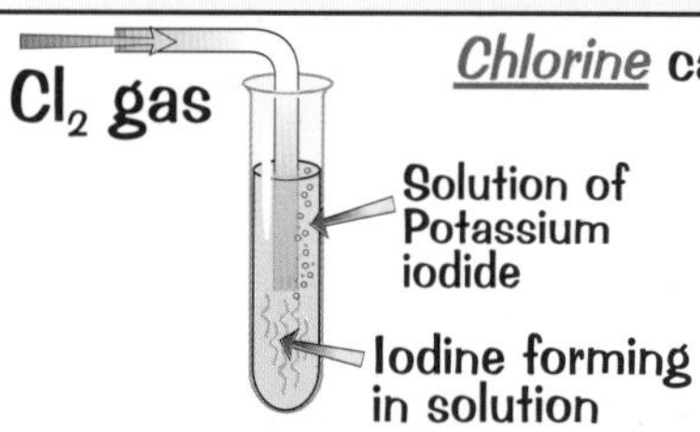

Cl_2 gas

Solution of Potassium iodide

Iodine forming in solution

Chlorine can displace _bromine_ and _iodine_ from a solution of _bromide_ or _iodide._

Bromine will also displace _iodine_ because of the _trend_ in _reactivity._

$$Cl_{2(g)} + 2KI_{(aq)} \rightarrow I_{2(aq)} + 2KCl_{(aq)}$$

$$Cl_{2(g)} + 2KBr_{(aq)} \rightarrow Br_{2(aq)} + 2KCl_{(aq)}$$

I've never liked Halogens — they give me a bad head...

Well, I think Halogens are just slightly less grim than the Alkali metals. At least they change colour and go from gases to liquid to solid. _Learn the boring facts anyway._ And smile ☺.

Uses of Halogens

Some Uses of Halogens you Really Should Know

Aren't halogens and their compounds ace. _Learn and enjoy._

Fluorine, (or rather fluoride) reduces dental decay

1) _Fluorides_ can be added to drinking water and toothpastes to help prevent _tooth decay_.

2) In its natural state fluorine appears as a _pale yellow gas_.

Chlorine is used in bleach and for sterilising water

1) _Chlorine_ dissolved in _sodium hydroxide_ solution is called _bleach_.

2) _Chlorine compounds_ are also used to _kill germs_ in swimming pools and drinking water.

3) It's used to make _insecticides_ and in the manufacture of _HCl_.

4) It's also used in the manufacture of the plastic PVC (polyvinyl _chloride_)

Iodine is used as an antiseptic...

...but it stings like nobody's business and stains the skin brown. Nice.

Silver halides are used on black and white photographic film

1) _Silver_ is very _unreactive_. It does form halides but they're very _easily_ split up.
2) In fact, ordinary visible _light_ has enough energy to do so.
3) _Photographic film_ is coated with _colourless silver bromide_.
4) When light hits parts of it, the silver bromide _splits up_ into _silver_ and _bromine_:

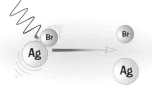

$$2AgBr \rightarrow Br_2 + 2Ag \text{ (silver metal)}$$

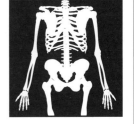

5) The _silver metal_ appears _black_. The brighter the light, the _darker_ it goes.
6) This produces a black and white _negative_, like an X-ray picture for example.

Hydrogen Halides dissolve to form Acidic Solutions

1) _Hydrogen halides_ are gases.
2) They _dissolve_ easily in water forming _strong acids_.
3) Halide gases _react with water_ to produce _halide ions_, which is what makes it _acidic_.
4) The _proper_ method for dissolving hydrogen halides in water is to use an _inverted funnel_ as shown:

Hydrogen Halide

$$HBr_{(g)} \xrightarrow{water} H^+_{(aq)} + Br^-_{(aq)}$$

$$HCl_{(g)} \xrightarrow{water} H^+_{(aq)} + Cl^-_{(aq)}$$

$$HI_{(g)} \xrightarrow{water} H^+_{(aq)} + I^-_{(aq)}$$

Well that's pretty much the bare bones of it anyway...

Lots of seriously tedious facts to learn here. And virtually no nonsense. But think about it, the only bit you're gonna really remember forever is that bit about iodine. _Am I right or am I right?_

Electrolysis of Salt

Salt is taken from the sea — and from underneath Cheshire

1) *Common salt* is a compound of *sodium* (an alkali metal) and *chloride* (a halogen).
2) It is found in large quantities in the *sea* and in *underground deposits*.
3) In *hot* countries they just pour *sea water* into big flat open *tanks* and let the *sun* evaporate the water to leave salt. This is no good in cold countries because there isn't enough sunshine.
4) In *Britain* (a cold country — as if you need reminding), salt is extracted from *underground deposits* left *millions* of years ago when *ancient seas* evaporated. There are massive deposits of this *ROCK SALT* in *Cheshire*.

Electrolysis of Salt gives Hydrogen, Chlorine and NaOH

Salt dissolved in water is called *BRINE*. When *concentrated brine* is *electrolysed* there are *three* useful products:

a) *Hydrogen gas* is given off at the cathode.
b) *Chlorine gas* is given off at the anode.
c) *Sodium hydroxide* is left in solution.

These are collected, and then used in all sorts of *industries* to make various products as detailed below.

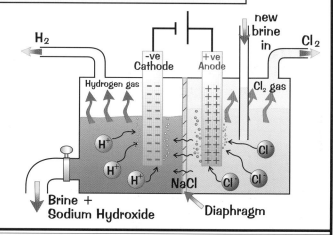

Useful Products from the Electrolysis of Brine

With all that effort and expense going into the electrolysis of brine, there'd better be some pretty useful stuff coming out of it — and so there is... and you have to learn it all too. Ace.

1) Chlorine

1) Used in *disinfectants* 2) *killing bacteria* (e.g. in *swimming pools*)
3) *plastics* 4) *HCl* 5) *insecticides*. Don't forget the simple lab test for chlorine — it *bleaches* damp *litmus paper*.

Damp Litmus Paper

2) Hydrogen

1) Used in the *Haber Process* to make *ammonia* (remember?).
2) Used to change *oils* into *fats* for making *margarine* ("hydrogenated vegetable oil"). Think about that when you spread it on your toast in the morning. Yum.

3) Sodium hydroxide

Sodium Hydroxide is a very strong *alkali* and is used *widely* in the *chemical industry*,
e.g. 1) *soap* 2) *ceramics* 3) *organic chemicals* 4) *paper pulp* 5) *oven cleaner*.

Learn the many uses of salt — just use your brine...

There's not much to learn on this page so you've got no excuse for not *learning it all*. Write down where salt is found and the products from the electrolysis of brine, suggesting a few uses for each one. Believe me, you won't get much easier marks in the Exam than these. Giveaway.

Chemical Equations

Equations need a lot of *practice* if you're going to get them right. They can get *real tricky* real quickly, unless you *really* know your stuff. Every time you do an equation you need to *practice* getting it *right* rather than skating over it.

Chemical formulae *tell you* how many atoms there are

1) Hydrogen chloride has the chemical formula HCl. This means that in any molecule of hydrogen chloride there will be: *one* atom of hydrogen bonded to *one* atom of chlorine.

2) Ammonia has the formula NH_3. This means that in any molecule of ammonia there will be: *three* atoms of hydrogen bonded to *one* atom of nitrogen. Simple.

3) A chemical reaction can be described by the process *reactants* → *products*.
   e.g.   methane *reacts* with oxygen to *produce* carbon dioxide and water
   e.g.   magnesium *reacts* with oxygen to *produce* magnesuim oxide.
   You have to know how to write these reactions in both words and symbols, as shown below:

The Symbol Equation *shows the atoms on both sides:*

Magnesium + Oxygen → Magnesium oxide
$$2Mg + O_2 → 2MgO$$

Methane + Oxygen → Water + Carbon Dioxide
$$CH_4 + 2O_2 → 2H_2O + CO_2$$

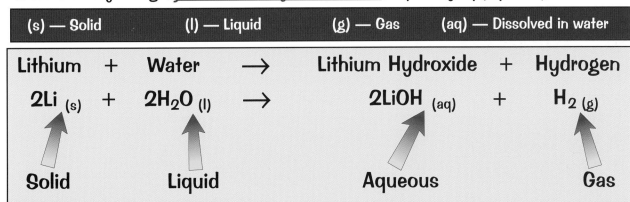

You need to know how to write out any Equation...

You *really* do need to know how to write out chemical equations. In fact you need to know how to write out equations for pretty well all the reactions in this book.

That might sound like an awful lot, but there aren't nearly as many as you think. Have a look.

You also need to know the *formulae* for all the *ionic* and *covalent* compounds in here too. Lovely.

State Symbols *tell you what Physical State it's in*

These are easy enough, *just make sure you know them*, especially aq (aqueous).

(s) — Solid	(l) — Liquid	(g) — Gas	(aq) — Dissolved in water

Lithium + Water → Lithium Hydroxide + Hydrogen
$$2Li_{(s)} + 2H_2O_{(l)} → 2LiOH_{(aq)} + H_{2(g)}$$

Solid   Liquid   Aqueous   Gas

It's tricky — but don't get yourself in a state over it...

Make sure you know the formulae for *all* the ionic and covalent compounds you've come across so far. And for *higher* level, write symbol equations for the following equations and put the state symbols in too: 1) Iron(III) oxide + hydrogen → iron + water
2) Dilute hydrochloric acid + aluminium → aluminium chloride + hydrogen (answers on P.106)

Balancing Equations

Things start to get a wee bit tricky now. Hang in there and remember... *practice makes perfect.*

Balancing The Equation — match them up one by one

1) There must always be the *same* number of atoms on *both sides*, they can't just *disappear.*
2) You *balance* the equation by putting numbers *IN FRONT* of the formulae where needed.
   Take this equation for reacting sulphuric acid with sodium hydroxide:

$$H_2SO_4 + NaOH \rightarrow Na_2SO_4 + H_2O$$

The *formulae* are all correct but the numbers of some atoms *don't match up* on both sides.
You *can't change formulae* like H_2SO_4 to H_2SO_5. You can only put numbers *in front of them*:

Method: Balance just ONE type of atom at a time

The more you practise, the quicker you get, but all you do is this:

1) Find an element that *doesn't balance* and *pencil in a number* to try and sort it out.
2) *See where it gets you.* It may create *another imbalance* but pencil in *another number* and see where that gets you.
3) Carry on chasing *unbalanced* elements and it'll *sort itself out* pretty quickly.

I'll show you. In the equation above you soon notice we're short of H atoms on the RHS.
1) The only thing you can do about that is make it $2H_2O$ instead of just H_2O:

$$H_2SO_4 + NaOH \rightarrow Na_2SO_4 + 2H_2O$$

2) But that now causes too many H atoms and O atoms on the RHS, so to balance that up you could try putting 2NaOH on the LHS (Left Hand Side):

$$H_2SO_4 + 2NaOH \rightarrow Na_2SO_4 + 2H_2O$$

3) And suddenly there it is! *Everything balances*. And you'll notice the Na just sorted itself out.

Electrolysis Equations — make sure the electrons balance

The main thing is to make sure the *number of electrons* is the *same* for *both half-equations.*
For the cell shown the basic half equations are:

CATHODE: $H^+_{(aq)} + e^- \rightarrow H$
ANODE: $Cl^-_{(aq)} \rightarrow Cl + e^-$

These equations *aren't finished* because both the hydrogen and the chlorine come off as *gases*. They must be *rewritten* with H_2 and Cl_2, like this:

CATHODE: $2H^+ + 2e^- \rightarrow H_{2(g)}$
ANODE: $2Cl^-_{(aq)} \rightarrow Cl_{2(g)} + 2e^-$

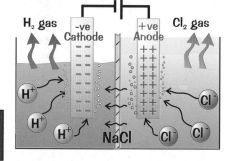

Note that there are *two electrons* in *both* half equations, which means they're nice and *balanced*. This gives the *OVERALL EQUATION*:

$$2HCl_{(aq)} \rightarrow H_{2(g)} + Cl_{2(g)}$$

Cations — sounds like a useful form of pet control...

Practise scribbling down all these details, *mini-essay* style. Electrolysis can be a bit confusing. I think you have to make an effort to learn all the details, especially how the two half equations are really just *one* equation, but it kind of happens in two places, *joined by a battery.*

Revision Summary for Module Eight

These certainly aren't the easiest questions you're going to come across. That's because they test what you know without giving you any clues. At first you might think they're impossibly difficult. Eventually you'll realise that they simply test whether you've learnt the stuff or not. If you're struggling to answer these then you need to do some serious learning.

1) Describe the bonding, atom spacing and physical properties for the three states of matter.
2) What are the three ways of changing between the three states of matter?
3) Explain what goes on all three processes, in terms of bonds and heat energy.
4) Sketch three gripping diffusion experiments and explain what happens in them.
5) Sketch and label a heating graph and a cooling graph. Explain why the graphs have flat spots.
6) Sketch an atom. Give five details about the nucleus and five details about the electrons.
7) What are the three particles found in an atom? What are their relative masses and charges?
8) What do the mass number and proton number represent?
9) Explain what an isotope is. Give a well-known example.
10) List five facts (or "Rules") about electron shells.
11) Calculate the electron configuration for each of the following elements: $^4_2$He, $^{12}_6$C, $^{31}_{15}$P, $^{39}_{19}$K.
12) What is the difference between elements, mixtures and compounds?
13) Give three examples for each of elements, mixtures and compounds.
14) What is ionic bonding? Which kind of atoms like to do ionic bonding? Why is this?
15) Draw a diagram of a giant ionic lattice and give three features of giant ionic structures.
16) List the three main properties of ionic compounds.
17) Which atoms form 1+, 1-, 2+ and 2- ions?
18) What is covalent bonding? Which kind of atoms tend to do covalent bonding? Why is this?
19) Why do some atoms do covalent bonding instead of ionic bonding?
20) Describe and draw diagrams to illustrate the bonding in: H_2, HCl, NH_3, CH_4 and H_2O.
21) What are the two types of covalent substances? Give three examples of each type.
22) Give three physical properties for each of the two types of covalent substance.
23) List the three main properties of metals and explain how the metallic bonding causes them.
24) Describe the difference between thermosoftening and thermosetting plastics.
25) What two properties did they base the early periodic table on?
26) Who was the old rogue who had the best shot at it and why was his table so clever?
27) What feature of atoms determines the order of the modern Periodic Table?
28) Draw diagrams to show the electron arrangements for the first twenty elements.
29) Explain the trend in reactivity of metals and non-metals using the notion of "shielding".
30) What are the electron arrangements of the noble gases? What are the properties of them?
31) List four physical properties, and two chemical properties of the alkali metals.
32) Give details of the reactions of the alkali metals with water and chlorine, and burning in air.
33) Describe the trends in appearance and reactivity of the halogens as you go down the Group.
34) List four properties common to all the halogens.
35) Give details, with equations, of the reaction of the halogens with metals, including silver.
36) Is hydrogen chloride covalent or ionic in its *natural* state? What about in acidic form?
37) List four properties of transition metals, and two properties of their compounds.
38) Why can graphite sometimes be used as a lubricant? Why is it used for pencil 'leads'?
39) Diamond and sand are both very hard. How come?
40) What is special about the bonding in metals?
41) What enables metals to conduct heat and electricity?
42) Draw a *detailed* diagram showing *clearly* how brine is electrolysed.
43) What are the two sources of salt and what are the three main uses of it?

Velocity and Acceleration

Speed and Velocity are Both just: HOW FAST YOU'RE GOING

Speed and velocity are both measured in *m/s* (or km/h or mph). They both simply say *how fast* you're going, but there's a *subtle difference* between them which *you need to know*:

SPEED is just *HOW FAST* you're going (e.g. 30mph or 20m/s) with no regard to the direction.
VELOCITY however must *ALSO* have the *DIRECTION* specified, e.g. 30mph *north* or 20m/s, 060°

Seems kinda fussy I know, but they expect you to remember that distinction, so there you go.

Speed, Distance and Time — the Formula:

$$\text{Speed} = \frac{\text{Distance}}{\text{Time}}$$

You really ought to get *pretty slick* with this *very easy formula*.
As usual the *formula triangle* version makes it all a bit of a *breeze*.
You just need to try and think up some interesting word for remembering the *order* of the *letters* in the triangle, s^{d}t.   Errm... sedit, perhaps... well, you think up your own.

EXAMPLE: A cat skulks 20m in 35s. Find   a) its speed   b) how long it takes to skulk 75m.
ANSWER: Using the formula triangle: a) s = d/t = 20/35 = <u>0.57m/s</u>
                                          b) t = d/s = 75/0.57 = 131s = <u>2mins 11sec</u>

A lot of the time we tend to use the words "speed" and "velocity" interchangeably.
For example to calculate velocity you'd just use the above formula for speed instead.

Acceleration is How Quickly You're Speeding Up

Acceleration is definitely *NOT* the same as *velocity* or *speed*.
    Every time you read or write the word *acceleration*, remind yourself: "*acceleration* is *COMPLETELY DIFFERENT* from *velocity*. Acceleration is how *quickly* the velocity is *changing*."
Velocity is a simple idea. Acceleration is altogether more *subtle*, which is why it's *confusing*.

Acceleration — The Formula:

$$\text{Acceleration} = \frac{\text{Change in Velocity}}{\text{Time Taken}}$$

Well, it's *just another formula*. Just like all the others. Three things in a *formula triangle*.
Mind you, there are *two* tricky things with this one. First there's the "ΔV", which means working out the *"change in velocity"*, as shown in the example below, rather than just putting a *simple value* for speed or velocity in.   Secondly there's the *units* of acceleration which are m/s^2.
Not m/s, which is *velocity*, but m/s^2. Got it? No?   Let's try once more: *Not m/s, but m/s^2*.

EXAMPLE: A skulking cat accelerates from 2m/s to 6m/s in 5.6s. Find its acceleration.
ANSWER: Using the formula triangle: a = ΔV/t = (6 - 2) / 5.6 = 4 ÷ 5.6 = <u>0.71 m/s^2</u>
            All pretty basic stuff I'd say.

Velocity and Acceleration — learn the difference...

It's true — some people don't realise that velocity and acceleration are totally different things.
Hard to believe I know — all part of the great mystery and tragedy of life I suppose.
Anyway. Learn the definitions and the formulae, *cover the page* and *scribble it all down again*.

D-T and V-T Graphs

Make sure you learn all these details real good. Make sure you can _distinguish_ between the two, too.

Distance-Time Graphs

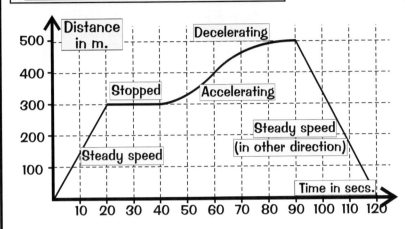

Very Important Notes:

1) _GRADIENT = SPEED_.
2) _Flat_ sections are where it's _stopped_.
3) The _steeper_ the graph, the _faster_ it's going.
4) _Downhill_ sections mean it's _coming back_ toward its starting point.
5) _Curves_ represent _acceleration_ or deceleration.
6) A _steepening_ curve means it's _speeding up_ (increasing gradient).
7) A _levelling off_ curve means it's _slowing down_ (decreasing gradient).

Calculating Speed _from a Distance-Time Graph — it's just the Gradient_

For example the _speed_ of the _return_ section of the graph is:

$Speed = gradient = \dfrac{vertical}{horizontal} = \dfrac{500}{30} = 16.7 \text{ m/s}$

Don't forget that you have to use the _scales_ of the axes to work out the gradient. _Don't_ measure in _cm_!

Velocity-Time Graphs

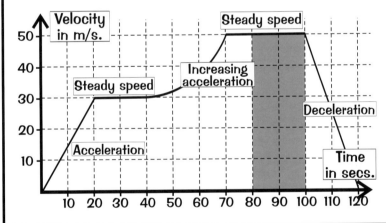

Very Important Notes:

1) _GRADIENT = ACCELERATION_.
2) _Flat_ sections represent _steady_ speed.
3) The _steeper_ the graph, the _greater_ the _acceleration_ or deceleration.
4) _Uphill_ sections (/) are _acceleration_.
5) _Downhill_ sections (\) — _deceleration_.
6) The _area_ under any section of the graph (or all of it) is equal to the _distance_ travelled in that _time_ interval.
7) A _curve_ means _changing acceleration_.

Calculating Acceleration, Speed _and Distance from a Velocity-time Graph_

1) The _ACCELERATION_ represented by the _first section_ of the graph is:

$Acceleration = gradient = \dfrac{vertical}{horizontal} = \dfrac{30}{20} = 1.5 \text{ m/s}^2$

2) The _SPEED_ at any point is simply found by _reading the value_ off the _speed axis_.
3) The _DISTANCE TRAVELLED_ in any time interval is equal to the _area_. For example, the distance travelled between t=80 and t=100 is equal to the _shaded area_ which is equal to _1000m_.

Understanding speed and stuff — it can be an uphill struggle...

The tricky thing about these two kinds of graph is that they can look pretty much the same but represent totally different kinds of motion. If you want to be able to do them (in the Exam) then there's no substitute for simply _learning all the numbered points_ for both types. Enjoy.

The Three Laws of Motion

Around about the time of the Great Plague in the 1660s, a chap called *Isaac Newton* worked out *The Three Laws of Motion*. At first they might seem kind of obscure or irrelevant, but to be perfectly blunt, if you can't understand these *three simple laws* then you'll never fully understand *forces and motion*:

First Law — *Balanced Forces* mean *No Change in Velocity*

> So long as the forces on an object are all *BALANCED*, then it'll just *STAY STILL*, or else if it's already moving it'll just carry on at the *SAME VELOCITY* — so long as the forces are all *BALANCED*.

1) When a train or car or bus or anything else is *moving* at a *constant velocity* then the *forces* on it must all be *BALANCED*.

2) Never let yourself entertain the *ridiculous idea* that things need a constant overall force to *keep* them moving — NO NO NO NO NO NO!

3) To keep going at a *steady speed*, there must be *ZERO RESULTANT FORCE* — and don't you forget it.

Second Law — *A Resultant Force* means *Acceleration*

> If there is an *UNBALANCED FORCE*, then the object will *ACCELERATE* in that direction.

1) An *unbalanced* force will always produce *acceleration* (or deceleration).

2) This *"acceleration"* can take *FIVE* different forms:
   Starting, *stopping*, *speeding up*, *slowing down* and *changing direction*.

3) On a force diagram, the *arrows* will be *unequal*:

Don't ever say: "If something's moving there must be an overall resultant force acting on it".

Not so. If there's an *overall* force it will always *accelerate*. You get *steady* speed from *balanced* forces. I wonder how many times I need to say that same thing before you remember it?

Three Points *Which Should Be Obvious:*

1) The bigger the *force*, the *GREATER* the *acceleration* or *deceleration*.
2) The bigger the *mass* the *SMALLER the acceleration*.
3) To get a *big* mass to accelerate *as fast* as a *small* mass it needs a *bigger* force.
   Just think about pushing *heavy* trolleys and it should all seem *fairly obvious*, I would hope.

The Overall Unbalanced Force is often called The Resultant Force

Any *resultant force* will produce *acceleration* and this is the *formula* for it:

$$F = ma \quad \text{or} \quad a = F/m$$

m = mass, a = acceleration F is always the *RESULTANT FORCE*

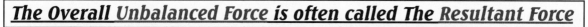

The Three Laws of Motion

Calculations using F = ma — An Example

Q) *What force is needed to accelerate a mass of 12kg at 5m/s² ?*

ANS. The question is asking for *force*

— so you need a formula with *"F = something-or-other"*.
Since they also give you values for *mass* and *acceleration*, the
formula *"F = ma"* really should be a *pretty obvious choice*, surely.
So just *stick* in the numbers they give you where the letters are:
m = 12, *a = 5*, so *"F = ma"* gives F = 12 × 5 = *60N* (It's *Newtons* because force always is)
(Notice that you don't really need to *fully understand* what's going on — you just need to know *how to use formulae*.)

The Third Law — Reaction Forces

> If object A *EXERTS A FORCE* on object B then object B
> exerts *THE EXACT OPPOSITE FORCE* on object A

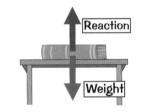

1) That means if you *push* against a wall, the wall will *push back* against you, *just as hard*.

2) And as soon as you *stop* pushing, *so does the wall*. Kinda clever really.

3) If you think about it, there must be an *opposing force* when you lean against a wall — otherwise you (and the wall) would *fall over*.

4) If you *pull* a cart, whatever force *you exert* on the rope, the rope exerts the *exact opposite* pull on *you*.

5) If you put a book on a table, the *weight* of the book acts *downwards* on the table, — and the table exerts an *equal and opposite* force *upwards* on the book.

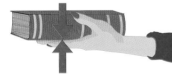

6) If you support a book on your *hand*, the book exerts its *weight* downwards on you, and you provide an *upwards* force on the book and it all stays nicely *in balance*.

In *Exam* questions they may well *test* this by getting you to fill in some *extra arrow* to represent the *reaction force*. Learn this *very important fact*:

> Whenever an object is on a horizontal *SURFACE*,
> there'll always be a *REACTION FORCE* pushing
> *UPWARDS*, supporting the object.
> The total *REACTION FORCE* will be *EQUAL*
> *AND OPPOSITE* to the weight.

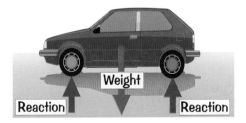

Hey, did you know — an unbalanced force causes ac...

Good old Isaac. Those three laws of motion are pretty inspirational don't you think? No? Oh.
Well you could do with learning them anyway, because in this topic there are hardly any nice
easy facts that'll help — in the end there's *no substitute* for fully understanding *The Three Laws*.

Weight & Force Diagrams

Gravity is the Force of Attraction Between All Masses

Gravity attracts _all_ masses, but you only notice it when one of the masses is _really really big_, i.e. a planet. Anything near a planet or star is _attracted_ to it _very strongly_. This has _two_ important effects:

1) It makes all things _accelerate_ towards the _ground_
   (all with the _same_ acceleration, g, which = _10m/s²_ on Earth).
2) It gives everything a _weight_.

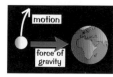

Weight and Mass are Not the Same

To understand this you must _learn all these facts_ about _mass and weight_.

1) _MASS_ is the _AMOUNT OF MATTER_ in an object.
   For any given object this will have the same value _ANYWHERE_ in the Universe.
2) _WEIGHT_ is caused by the _pull_ of gravity. In most questions the _weight_ of an object is just the _force_ of gravity pulling it towards the centre of the _Earth_.
3) One very fancy definition of a _Newton_. You need to know it.

ONE NEWTON is the force needed to give a **MASS OF 1 kg** an **ACCELERATION OF 1m/s²**

The Very Important Formula relating Mass, Weight and Gravity

$$W = m \times g$$

(Weight = mass × g)

1) Remember, weight and mass are _NOT the same_. Mass is in _kg_, weight is in _Newtons_.
2) The letter "_g_" represents the _strength_ of the gravity and its value is _different_ for _different planets_.
   On Earth g = 10 N/kg. _On the Moon_, where the gravity is weaker, g is just 1.6 N/kg.

Force Diagrams

There are basically only _A FEW DIFFERENT FORCE DIAGRAMS_ you can get:

1) Stationary Object — All Forces in Balance

1) The force of _GRAVITY_ (or weight) is acting _downwards_.
2) This causes a _REACTION FORCE_ from the surface _pushing_ the object _back up_.
3) This is the _only way_ it can be in _BALANCE_.
4) _Without_ a reaction force, it would accelerate _downwards_ due to the pull of gravity.
5) The two _HORIZONTAL forces_ must be _equal and opposite_ otherwise the object will accelerate _sideways_.

2) Steady Velocity — All Forces in Balance!

TAKE NOTE! To move with a _steady speed_ the forces must be in _BALANCE_. If there is an _unbalanced force_ then you get _ACCELERATION_, not steady speed. That's _rrrreal important_ so don't forget it.

3) Acceleration — Unbalanced Forces

1) You only get _acceleration_ with an overall _resultant_ (unbalanced) _force_.
2) The _bigger_ this _unbalanced force_, the _greater_ the _acceleration_.
3) Note that the forces in the _other direction_ are still _balanced_.

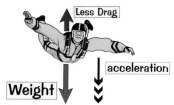

Learn about gravity NOW — no point in "weighting" around...

Very often, the only way to "_understand_" something is to _learn all the facts about it_. That's certainly true here. "Understanding" the difference between mass and weight is no more than learning all those facts about them. When you've learnt all those facts, you'll understand it.

Friction & Terminal Velocity

1) Friction is Always There to Slow things Down

1) If an object has _no force_ propelling it along it will always _slow down and stop_ because of _friction_.
2) Friction always acts in the _opposite_ direction to movement.
3) To travel at a _steady_ speed, the driving force needs to _balance_ the frictional forces.
4) Friction occurs in _TWO_ main ways:

a) FRICTION *BETWEEN* SOLID SURFACES *WHICH ARE* SLIDING PAST EACH OTHER

For example between _brake pads and brake discs_. There's just as much force of _friction_ here as between the tyres and the road. In fact in the end, if you brake hard enough the friction here becomes _greater_ than at the tyres, and then the wheel _skids_.

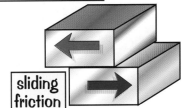

sliding friction

b) RESISTANCE *OR* "DRAG" *FROM FLUIDS* (AIR *OR* LIQUID)

The most important factor _by far_ in _reducing drag_ in fluids is keeping the shape of the object _streamlined_, like fish bodies or boat hulls or bird wings/bodies. The _opposite_ extreme is a _parachute_ which is about as _high drag_ as you can get — which is, of course, _the whole idea_.

2) But We Also Need Friction to Move and to Stop!

It's easy to think of friction as generally a _nuisance_ because we always seem to be working _against it_, but don't forget that _without it_ we wouldn't be able to _walk_ or _run_ or go _sky-diving_ etc. It also holds _nuts and bolts_ together.

3) Friction Causes Wear and Heating

1) Friction acts between _surfaces_ that are _sliding past_ each other. _Machinery_ has lots of surfaces doing that.
2) Friction always produces _heat_ and _wearing_ of the surfaces.
3) _Lubricants_ keep the friction _low_ and thus reduce wear.

Lubrication needed here
Bearings
Bearings
Rotating shaft

Cars and Free-Fallers all Reach a Terminal Velocity

When cars and free-falling objects first _set off_ they have _much more_ force _accelerating_ them than _resistance_ slowing them down. As the _speed_ increases the resistance _builds up_. This gradually _reduces_ the _acceleration_ until eventually the _resistance force_ is _equal_ to the _accelerating force_ and then it won't be able to accelerate any more. It will have reached its maximum speed or _TERMINAL VELOCITY_.

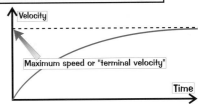

Velocity
Maximum speed or "terminal velocity"
Time

resistance
weight

resistance
weight

The most important example is the human _skydiver_. Without his parachute open he has quite a _small_ area and a force of "_W=mg_" pulling him down. He reaches a _terminal velocity_ of about _120mph_.
But with the parachute _open_, there's much more _air resistance_ (at any given speed) and still only the same force "_W=mg_" pulling him down.
This means his _terminal velocity_ comes right down to about _15mph_, which is a _safe speed_ to hit the ground at.

Learn about friction — just don't let it wear you down...

I would never have thought there was so much to say about friction. Nevertheless, there it all is, all mentioned in the NEAB syllabus, and all very likely to come up in your Exam. Ignore it at your peril. _Learn_ the six main headings, then the stuff, then _cover the page_ and away you go.

Stopping Distances For Cars

They're pretty keen on this for Exam questions, so make sure you _learn it properly_.

The Many Factors Which Affect Your Total Stopping Distance

The distance it takes to stop a car is divided into the _THINKING DISTANCE_ and the _BRAKING DISTANCE_.

1) Thinking Distance

"The distance the car travels in the split-second between a hazard appearing and the driver applying the brakes".

It's affected by _THREE MAIN FACTORS_:

a) _How FAST you're going_ — obviously. Whatever your reaction time, the _faster_ you're going, the _further_ you'll go.

b) _How DOPEY you are_ — This is affected by _tiredness_, _drugs_, _alcohol_, _old-age_, and a _careless_ blasé attitude.

c) _How BAD the VISIBILITY is_ — lashing rain and oncoming lights, etc. make _hazards_ harder to spot.

2) Braking Distance

"The distance the car travels during its deceleration whilst the brakes are being applied."

It's affected by _FOUR MAIN FACTORS_:

a) _How FAST you're going_ — obviously. The _faster_ you're going the _further_ it takes to stop (see below).

b) _How HEAVILY LOADED the vehicle is_ — with the _same_ brakes, _a heavily-laden_ vehicle takes _longer to stop_. A car won't stop as quick when it's full of people and luggage and towing a caravan.

c) _How good your BRAKES are_ — all brakes must be checked and maintained _regularly_. Worn or faulty brakes will let you down _catastrophically_ just when you need them the _most_, i.e. in an _emergency_.

d) _How good the GRIP is_ — this depends on _THREE THINGS_:
1) _road surface_, 2) _weather_ conditions, 3) _tyres_.

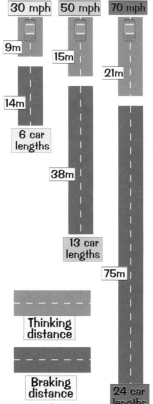

The figures below for typical stopping distances are from the Highway code. It's frightening to see just how far it takes to stop when you're going at 70mph.

Leaves and diesel spills and muck on t'road are _serious hazards_ because they're _unexpected_. _Wet_ or _icy roads_ are always much more _slippy_ than dry roads, but often you only discover this when you try to _brake_ hard! Tyres should have a minimum _tread depth_ of _1.6mm_. This is essential for getting rid of the _water_ in wet conditions. Without _tread_, a tyre will simply _ride_ on a _layer of water_ and skid _very easily_. This is called "_aquaplaning_" and isn't nearly as cool as it sounds.

Resultant Force is Real Important — Especially for "F = ma"

In most _real_ situations there are at least _two forces_ acting on an object along any direction. The _overall_ effect of these forces will decide the _motion_ of the object — whether it will _accelerate_, _decelerate_ or stay at a _steady speed_. The "_overall effect_" is found by just _adding or subtracting_ the forces which point along the _same_ direction. The overall force you get is called the _RESULTANT FORCE_. And when you use the _formula_ "_F = ma_", F must always be the _RESULTANT FORCE_.

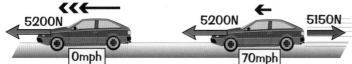

Car at 0mph:
Resultant force = 5,200N

Car at 70mph:
Resultant force = 5,200 – 5,150 = 50N

Muck on t'road, eh — by gum, it's grim up North...

They mention this specifically in the syllabus and are very likely to test you on it since it involves safety. Learn all the details and write yourself a _mini-essay_ to see how much you _really know_.

Work Done and Kinetic Energy

When a *force* moves an *object*, *ENERGY IS TRANSFERRED* and *WORK IS DONE*

That statement sounds far more complicated than it needs to. Try this:

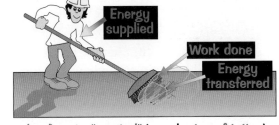

1) Whenever something *moves*, something else is providing some sort of *"effort"* to move it.
2) The thing putting the *effort* in needs a *supply* of energy (like *fuel* or *food* or *electricity* etc.).
3) It then does *"work"* by *moving* the object — and one way or another it *transfers* the energy it receives (as fuel) into *other forms*.
4) Whether this energy is transferred *"usefully"* (e.g. by *lifting a load*) or is *"wasted"* (e.g. lost as *friction*), you can still say that *"work is done"*. Just like Batman and Bruce Wayne, *"work done"* and *"energy transferred"* are indeed *"one and the same"*. (And they're both in *Joules*)

It's Just Another Trivial Formula:

Work Done = Force × Distance

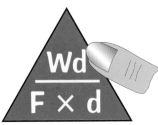

Whether the force is *friction* or *weight* or *tension in a rope*, it's always the same. To find how much *energy* has been *transferred* (in Joules), you just multiply the *force in N* by the *distance moved in m*. Easy as that. I'll show you...

EXAMPLE: Some hooligan kids drag an old tractor tyre 5m over rough ground. They pull with a total force of 340N. Find the energy transferred.

ANSWER: Wd = F×d = 340 × 5 = <u>1700J</u>.   *Phew — easy peasy isn't it?*

Kinetic Energy is Energy of Movement

Anything which is *moving* has *kinetic energy*.
The *kinetic energy* of something depends both on *MASS* and *SPEED*.
The *more* it weighs and the *faster* it's going, the *bigger* its kinetic energy will be.

There's a *slightly tricky* formula for it, so you have to concentrate *a little bit harder* for this one. But hey, that's life — it can be real tough sometimes:

Kinetic Energy = ½ × mass × velocity^2

K.E. ½ × m × v^2

EXAMPLE: A car of mass 2450kg is travelling at 38m/s. Calculate its kinetic energy.

ANSWER: It's pretty easy. You just plug the numbers into the formula but watch the *"V²"* !
KE = ½ m v^2 = ½ × 2450 × 38^2 = <u>1 768 900J</u> (*Joules* because it's *energy*)

(When the car stops suddenly, all this energy is dissipated as heat at the brakes — it's a lot of heat)

small mass, not fast low kinetic energy

big fast lorries Ltd

big mass, real fast high kinetic energy

Revise work done — what else...

"Energy transferred" and *"work done"* are the same thing. I wonder how many times I need to say that before you'll remember. Power is *"work done divided by time taken"*. I wonder how many times you've got to see that before you realise you're supposed to *learn it* as well...

Stretching Springs

Stretching Springs — Extension is Proportional to Load

This is _seriously easy_. It just means:

> If you _STRETCH_ something with a _STEADILY INCREASING FORCE_, then the _LENGTH_ will _INCREASE STEADILY_ too.

The important thing to measure in a stretching experiment is not so much the total length as the _EXTENSION_.

> _EXTENSION_ is the _INCREASE IN LENGTH_ compared to the original length with _no force applied_.

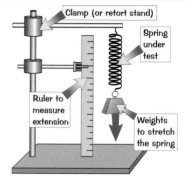

For most materials, you'll find that _THE EXTENSION IS PROPORTIONAL TO THE LOAD_, which just means if you _double_ the load, the _extension is doubled too_.

The behaviour of the spring changes at the elastic limit:

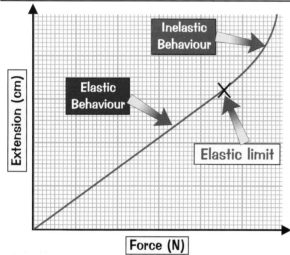

Region 1 — Elastic behaviour

1) In this region when the load is _doubled_ the extension _doubles too_.
2) The spring will _always return_ to its original _size and shape_ when the load is removed.

Region 2 — The Elastic Limit

1) The _elastic limit_. This is the point at which the behaviour of the spring suddenly changes.
2) _Below_ this point the spring _keeps_ its original _size and shape_.
3) _Above_ this point the spring behaves _inelastically_.

Region 3 — Inelastic behaviour

1) In this region the spring _doesn't return_ to its original _size and shape_ when the load is _removed_.
2) The extension no longer doubles when the load is doubled.

If you put _too much_ load on the spring then it will be _permanently damaged_.

You should **LEARN** that this always gives _A STRAIGHT LINE GRAPH THROUGH THE ORIGIN_.

Elastic Potential Energy is Energy Stored in Springs

Elastic potential energy is the energy _stored_ when _work is done on an object_ to distort it.
If a spring is either _compressed_ or _stretched_ then it is said to have _elastic potential energy_.

Stretching Springs — always loads of fun...

This is pretty standard stuff, so make sure you know all the little details, including the graph, and the ideas behind the straight bits and curved bits. Also make sure you know about the three regions of the graph. Then find out what you know: _cover, scribble, check, etc._

Pressure on Surfaces

Pressure is not the same as Force

Too many people get *force* and *pressure* mixed up — but there's a *pretty serious difference* between them.

PRESSURE is defined as the *FORCE ACTING* on *UNIT AREA* of a surface

Now read on, learn, and squirm with pleasure as another great mystery of the Physical Universe is exposed to your numb and weary mind...

Force vs Pressure *has a lot to do with* Damaging Surfaces

A force concentrated in a *small area* creates a *high pressure* — which means that the thing will *sink* into the surface. But with a *big* area, you get a *low* pressure which means it *doesn't* sink into the surface.

A Force *Spread over a Big Area* means Low Pressure *and No Sinking*

Foundations   Snow shoes   Tractor tyres   Drawing pins

A Force *Concentrated on a Small Area* means High Pressure *and Damage*

Ice skates   Stiletto heels   Sharp knives   Drawing pins

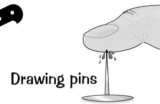

Pressure in Liquids *Acts in All Directions* and Increases With Depth

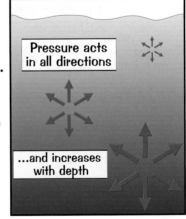

1) In a *gas* or *liquid* the same pressure acts outwards in *all* directions. This is *different* from solids which transmit forces in *one direction only*.

2) Also, the *pressure* in a liquid or gas *increases* as you go *deeper*. This is due to the *weight* of all the stuff *above it* pushing down. Imagine the weight of all the water *directly* over you at a depth of 100m. All of that is *pushing down* on the water below and *increasing the pressure* down there. This is what *limits* the depth that submarines can go to before the pressure *crushes* the hull or bursts through a weak join somewhere.

3) The *increase* in pressure also depends on the *density* of the fluid. Air is *not very dense*, so air pressure changes *relatively little* as you go up through the atmosphere. Water *is* pretty dense though, so the pressure increases very quickly as you go *deeper*.

Pressure acts in all directions

...and increases with depth

Spread the load and reduce the pressure — start revising now...

It's funny old stuff is pressure. Force is a nice easy concept and people usually do fine with it. But pressure is just that bit trickier — and that means it can cause people a lot of gip. Make sure you *learn all these details* about pressure. They're all worth marks in the Exam.

Pressure = Force / Area

$$\text{Pressure} = \frac{\text{Force}}{\text{Area}}$$

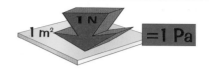

The normal _unit of pressure_ is the _Pascal_, Pa, which is the same as N/m². There is a fancy definition of the Pascal. If you think it helps, you can learn it:

A pressure of _ONE PASCAL_ is exerted by a _FORCE OF 1N_ acting at right angles to an _AREA of 1m²_

They may well give you questions with areas given in _cm²_. Don't try to _convert cm² to m²_ which is a bit tricky. Instead, just work out the pressure using P = F/A in the normal way, but give the answer as N/cm² rather than N/m² (Pa). Do remember that _N/cm²_ is _not_ the same as Pascals (which are N/m²).

Hydraulics — the Main Application of "P = F/A"

Hydraulic systems all use _two important features_ of _pressure in liquids_. _LEARN THEM_:

> 1) **PRESSURE IS _TRANSMITTED THROUGHOUT THE LIQUID_**, so that the force can easily be applied **_WHEREVER YOU WANT IT_**, using flexible pipes.
>
> 2) The force can be **_MULTIPLIED_** according to the **_AREAS_** of the pistons used.

Hydraulic Jack

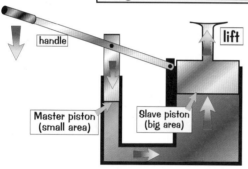

Car Brakes

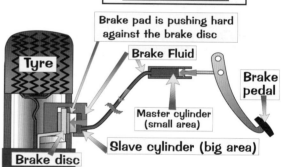

1) All hydraulic systems use a _SMALL master piston_ and a _BIG slave piston_.
2) The _master piston_ is used to apply a _force_ which puts the liquid _under pressure_.
3) This pressure is _transmitted_ throughout _all_ the liquid in the system, and somewhere _at the other end_ it pushes on the _slave piston_ which _exerts a force_ where it's needed.
4) The _slave piston_ always has a _much larger area_ than the _master piston_ so that it exerts a _much greater force_ from the pressure created by the force on the master piston. Clever stuff.
5) In this way, _hydraulic systems_ are used as _force multipliers_. i.e. they use a _small force_ to create a _very big force_ — a nice trick if you can do it.

The Typical Method for the Typical Exam Question:

1) Use the _master cylinder area_ and _force_ to calculate **THE PRESSURE IN THE SYSTEM**, P = F/A
2) Apply this pressure to the _area of the slave piston_ to calculate the **FORCE EXERTED**, F = P×A

EXAMPLE: The car master piston has an area of 4cm². If a force of 400N is applied to it, calculate the pressure created in the brake pipes. If the slave piston has an area of 40cm², calculate the force exerted on the brake disc.

ANSWER: At the _master piston:_ Pressure created = F/A = 400N÷4cm² = <u>100N/cm²</u> (Not Pascals!)
At the _slave piston:_ Force produced = P×A = 100×40 = <u>4000</u> (10 times original force)

Learn about hydraulics — and make light work of it...

You certainly need to know that formula for pressure, but that's pretty easy. The really tricky bit which you need to concentrate most on is how that formula is applied (twice) to explain how hydraulic systems turn a small force into a big one. _Keep working at it till you understand it._

Pressure in Gases

Volume is *Inversely Proportional to Pressure*

This sounds a lot more confusing than it actually is. Here is the fancy definition:

> When the *PRESSURE IS INCREASED* on a *fixed mass of gas* kept at *constant temperature*, the *VOLUME WILL DECREASE*. The changes in pressure and volume are in *INVERSE PROPORTION*.

If you ask me it's a pretty *obvious* way for a gas to behave. In simple language it's just this:

> If you squash a gas into a smaller space, the pressure goes up in proportion to how much you squash it. e.g. if you squash it to half the amount of space, it'll end up at twice the pressure it was before (so long as you don't let it get hotter or colder, or let any escape). Simple, innit?

It can work *both ways* too. If you *increase the PRESSURE*, the *volume must DECREASE*. If you *increase the VOLUME*, the *pressure must DECREASE*. That's all pretty obvious though isn't it?

Gas Syringe Experiments Are Good For Showing this Law

1) A *gas syringe* makes a pretty good *airtight seal* and is great for demonstrating this law.

2) You put *weights on the top* to give a *definite* known force pushing down on the piston.

3) If you *double the weight*, you also double the *force* which doubles the *pressure*.

4) You can then measure the *volume change* using the *scale* on the side of the syringe. Easy peasy.

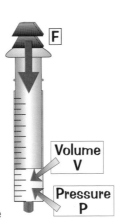

Using the Formula "$P_1V_1 = P_2V_2$"

Well what can I say, it's another formula. Not quite one you can put in a triangle, but still the same old idea: *stick in the numbers* they give you, and *work out the value* for the remaining letter. Please try and get it into your head that you don't need to *fully understand* the Physics, you just need a bit of "common sense" about *formulae*. Understanding always helps of course, but you can still get the right answer without it! Really, you've just got to identify the values for each letter — the rest is *very routine*.

EXAMPLE: A gas is compressed from a volume of 300cm³ at a pressure of 2.5 atmospheres down to a volume of 175cm³. Find the new pressure, *in atmospheres*.

ANSWER: "$P_1V_1 = P_2V_2$" gives: $2.5 \times 300 = P_2 \times 175$, so $P_2 = (2.5 \times 300) \div 175 = 4.3$ atm.

NB For *this formula*, always keep the units *the same* as they give them (in this case, pressure in *atmospheres*)

Less space, more collisions, more pressure — just like London...

This is another topic that can seem a lot more confusing than it really is. The basic principle of the law is simple enough, and so is the Gas Syringe demo. The formula might look bad but really there's nothing to it. In the end it's just stuff that needs *learning*, that's all. *Scribble*.

The Cause of Days and Seasons

The Rotation of The Earth Causes Day and Night

1) As the Earth slowly _rotates_ any point on the Earth's surface moves from the _bright side_ in the _sunlight_ round into the _darkness_. As the Earth keeps rotating it eventually comes back into the sunshine again.

   This sequence describes _day-dusk-night-dawn_.

2) A _full rotation_ takes _24 hours_ of course — a full day. Next time you watch the _Sun set_, try to _imagine yourself_ helpless on that _big rotating ball_ as you move silently across the _twilight zone_ and into the _shadows_.

3) Also notice that because of the _tilt_ of the axis, places in the _Northern Hemisphere_ are spending _much longer_ in the _sunshine_ than in the _shade_ (night time), whereas places in the _Southern Hemisphere_ are spending more time in the _dark_. This is only because of the _time of year_. See below.

4) Also notice that the further towards the _Poles_ you get, the _longer_ the days are in _summer_ and the longer the _nights_ are in _winter_. Places _inside_ the _arctic circle_ have _24 hours a day_ of sunlight for a few days in _mid summer_, whilst in _mid winter_ the Sun _never rises_ at all.

5) At the _Equator_ by contrast, the length of day _never varies_ from one season to the next. It's always _12 hours of day_ and _12 hours of night_. The position of the _shadows_ shows all this.

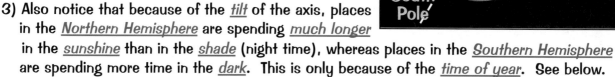

The Orbit of the Earth around the Sun takes 365¼ days

One _full orbit_ of the Earth around the Sun is _approximately 365 days_ (One year).
This is split up into _the seasons_:

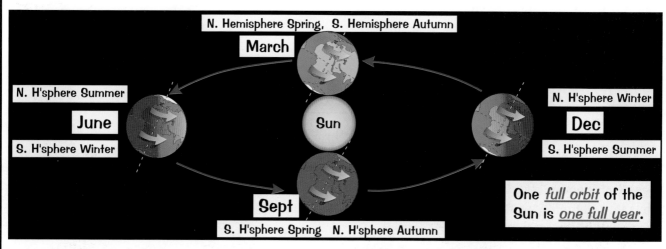

In the dim and distant past _early astronomers_ thought that the Sun and all the planets _orbited the Earth_. i.e. that the Earth was the _centre of the Universe_.
As we all know this was _very wrong_, but then they also thought the Earth was flat, and that the moon was made of cheese.

See Norway at Christmas — take a good torch...

This stuff about what causes the Sun to seem to "rise" and "set" and how the seasons are caused is surely irresistible-just-gotta-know-all-about-it kind of information, isn't it? Surely you must be filled with burning curiosity about it every time the dawn breaks — aren't you?

The Solar System

The _order_ of the planets can be remembered by using the little jollyism below:

Mercury,	Venus,	Earth,	Mars,	(Asteroids),	Jupiter,	Saturn,	Uranus,	Neptune,	Pluto
(My	Very	Energetic	Maiden	Aunt	Just	Swam	Under	North	Pier)

MERCURY, _VENUS_, _EARTH_ and _MARS_ are known as the _INNER PLANETS_.
JUPITER, _SATURN_, _URANUS_, _NEPTUNE_ and _PLUTO_ are much further away and are the _OUTER PLANETS_.

The Planets Don't Give Out Light, They just Reflect The Sun's

1) You can _see_ some of the nearer planets with the _naked eye_ at night, e.g. Mars and Venus.
2) They look just like _stars_, but they are of course _totally different_.
3) Stars are _huge_ and _very far away_ and _give out_ lots of light.
   The planets are _smaller and nearer_ and they just _reflect the sunlight_ falling on them.
4) Planets always _orbit around stars_. In our Solar System the planets orbit the _Sun_ of course.
5) These orbits are all _slightly elliptical_ (elongated circles).
6) All the planets in our Solar System orbit in the _same plane_ except Pluto (as shown).

The Sun is a Star, Giving Out All Types of EM Radiation

1) The Sun, like other stars produces _heat_ from _nuclear fusion reactions_ which turn
   hydrogen into helium. This makes it really hot.
2) It gives out the _full spectrum_ of _electromagnetic radiation_.

Sun

The Relative Sizes of the Planets and Sun

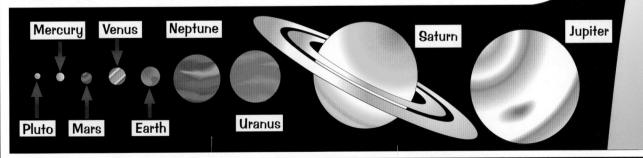

Learn The Planets — they can be quite illuminating...

Isn't the Solar System great! All those pretty coloured planets and all that big black empty
space. You can look forward to one or two easy questions on the planets — or you might get
two real horrors instead. Be ready, _learn_ all the _nitty gritty details_ till you know it all real good.

The Planets

Some Data on Planets which you Need to Kind of Know About

That doesn't mean you should learn every number, but you should definitely have a pretty good idea which planets are biggest, or furthest out etc. This table is a summary of the most important data on planets:

	PLANET	DIAMETER (km)	MASS		MEAN DIST. FROM SUN		ORBIT TIME	
INNER PLANETS	MERCURY	4 800	0.05		58		88d	
	VENUS	12 100	0.8	(Earth	108	(millions	225d	d=Earth
	EARTH	12 800	1.0	masses)	150	of km)	365d	days
	MARS	6 800	0.1		228		687d	
OUTER PLANETS	JUPITER	143 000	318.0		778		12y	
	SATURN	120 000	95.0		1430		29y	y=Earth
	URANUS	51 000	15.0		2870		84y	years
	NEPTUNE	49 000	17.0		4500		165y	
	PLUTO	2 400	0.003		5900		248y	

Gravity Is the Force which Keeps Everything in Orbit

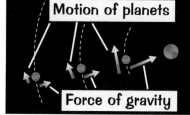

Motion of planets

Force of gravity

1) _Gravity_ is a force of _attraction_ which acts between _all_ masses.
2) With _very large_ masses like _stars_ and _planets_, the force is _very big_ and acts _a long way out_.
3) The _closer_ you get to a planet, the _stronger_ the _force of attraction_.
4) To _counteract_ this stronger gravity, the planet must move _faster_ and cover its orbit _quicker_.
5) _Comets_ are also held in _orbit_ by gravity, as are _moons_ and _satellites_ and _space stations_.

Planets in the Night Sky Seem to Move across the Constellations

1) The stars in the sky form _fixed patterns_ called _constellations_.
2) These all stay _fixed_ in _relation to each other_ and simply "_rotate_" as the Earth spins.
3) The _planets_ look _just like stars_ except that they _wander_ across the constellations over periods of _days or weeks_, often going in the _opposite direction_.
4) Their position and movement depends on where they are _in their orbit_, compared to us.
5) This _peculiar movement_ of the planets made the early astronomers realise that the Earth _wasn't the centre of the Universe_ after all, but was in fact just _the third rock from the Sun_. It's _very strong evidence_ for the _Sun-centred_ model of the Solar System.
6) Alas, the boys at _The Spanish Inquisition_ were less than keen on such heresy, and poor old _Copernicus_ had a pretty hard time of it for a while. In the end though, "_the truth will out_".

Learn This Page — but keep shtum to the boys in the Red Robes...

Planets are ace aren't they. There's all that exciting data to sort of be vaguely familiar with for a start. Then there's the fact that you can see one or two of them in the night sky, just by lifting your eyes to the heavens. _Learn_ all the other details on this page too, then _cover and scribble_.

Satellites

All satellites _in orbit_ about a body, be they artificial or natural, have to move at a _certain speed_ to stay in orbit at a _certain distance_. The _greater_ the distance away the _longer_ it takes to complete a _full orbit_. This also means that the _further_ away then the _slower_ the satellite must travel to _maintain its orbit_.

1) _Moons_ are sometimes called _Natural Satellites_

The planets in our solar system are all _natural satellites_ of the Sun. The planets also have their own natural satellites (moons):

2) _Artificial Satellites are very useful_

Artificial satellites are sent up by humans for _four main purposes_:

1) Monitoring _Weather_.
2) _Communications_, e.g. phone and TV.
3) _Space research_ such as the Hubble Telescope.
4) _Spying_ on baddies.

There are _two different orbits_ useful for satellites:

3) _Geostationary Satellites are Used For Communications_

1) These can also be called _geosynchronous satellites_.
2) They are put in _quite a high orbit_ over the _Equator_ which takes _exactly 24 hours_ to complete.
3) This means that they _stay above the same point_ on the Earth's surface because the Earth _rotates with them_ — hence the name Geo-(Earth)stationary.
4) This makes them _ideal_ for _Telephone and TV_ because they're always in the _same place_ and they can _transfer signals_ from one side of the Earth to another in a _fraction of a second_.

4) _Low Polar Orbit Satellites are for Weather and Spying_

1) In a _low polar orbit_ the satellite sweeps over _both poles_ whilst the Earth _rotates beneath it_.
2) The time taken for each full orbit is just _a few hours_.
3) Each time the satellite comes round it can _scan_ the next bit of the globe.
4) This allows the _whole surface_ of the planet to be _monitored_ each day.
5) Geostationary satellites are _too high_ to take good weather or spying photos, but the satellites in _polar orbits_ are _nice and low_.

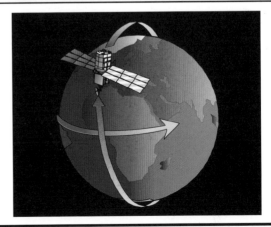

Learn about Satellites — and look down on your friends...

You can actually see the low polar orbit satellites on a nice dark clear night. They look like stars except they move quite fast in a dead straight line across the sky. You're never gonna spot the geostationary ones though! _Learn all the details_ about satellites, ready for seizing juicy marks.

The Universe

Stars and Solar Systems form from Clouds of Dust

1) _Stars form_ from _clouds of dust_ which _spiral in together_ due to _gravitational attraction_.

2) The gravity _compresses_ the matter so much that _intense heat_ develops and sets off _nuclear fusion reactions_ and the star then begins _emitting light_ and _other radiation_.

3) At the _same time_ that the star is forming, _other lumps_ may develop in the _spiralling dust clouds_ and these eventually gather together and form _planets_ which orbit _around the star_.

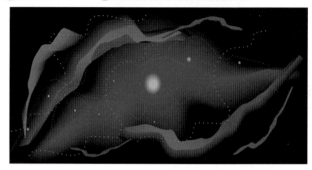

Our Sun is in The Milky Way Galaxy

1) The _Sun_ is one of _many millions_ of _stars_ which form the _Milky Way galaxy_.

2) The _distance_ between neighbouring stars is usually _millions of times greater_ than the distance between _planets_ in our Solar System. The Milky Way is _100,000 light years_ across.

3) The _nearest star_ to us (apart from the Sun of course) is _4.2 light years_ away.

4) _Gravity_ is of course the _force_ which keeps the stars _together_ in a _galaxy_ and, like most things in the Universe, the galaxies _all rotate_, kinda like a catherine wheel only _much slower_.

You are here

5) Our Sun is out towards the _end_ of one of the _spiral arms_ of the Milky Way galaxy.

The Whole Universe has More Than A Billion Galaxies

You are here

1) _Galaxies_ themselves are often _millions of times further apart_ than the _stars are_ within a galaxy. So that's 4.2 _million_ light years apart.

2) So even the slowest amongst you will soon begin to realise that the Universe is _mostly empty space_ and is _really really big_. Ever been to the NEC? Yeah? Well, it's even bigger than that.

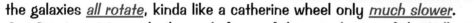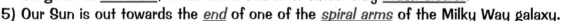

Galaxies, The Milky Way — it's just like a big chocolate factory...

More gripping facts about the Universe. It's just so big — look at those numbers: 1 light year is _9½ million million km_, one galaxy is _100,000_ of those across, and the Universe contains _billions_ of galaxies, all _millions_ of times further apart than 100,000 light years is. Man, _that's real big_.

The Life Cycle of Stars

Stars go through _many traumatic stages_ in their lives — just like teenagers.

Clouds of Dust and Gas

1) Stars _initially form_ from clouds of _DUST AND GAS_.

Protostar

2) The _force of gravity_ makes the dust particles come _spiralling in together_. As they do, _gravitational energy_ is converted into _heat energy_ and the _temperature rises_.

Main Sequence Star

3) When the _temperature_ gets _high enough_, _hydrogen nuclei_ undergo _nuclear fusion_ to form _helium nuclei_ and give out massive amounts of _heat and light_. A star is born. It immediately enters a long _stable period_ where the _heat created_ by the nuclear fusion provides an _outward pressure_ to _BALANCE_ the _force of gravity_ pulling everything _inwards_. In this stable period it's called a _MAIN SEQUENCE STAR_ and it lasts about _10 billion years_. (So the _Earth_ has already had _HALF its innings_ before the Sun _engulfs_ it!)

Red Giant

4) Eventually the _hydrogen_ begins to _run out_ and the star then _swells_ into a _RED GIANT_. It becomes _red_ because the surface _cools_.

5) A _SMALL STAR_ like our Sun will then begin to _cool_ and _contract_ into a _WHITE DWARF_ and then finally, as the light _fades completely_, it becomes a _BLACK DWARF_. (That's going to be really sad.)

Small stars → **White Dwarf** → **Black Dwarf**

Big stars

6) _BIG STARS_ however, start to _glow brightly again_ as they undergo more _fusion_ and _expand and contract several times_ forming _heavier elements_ in various _nuclear reactions_. Eventually they _explode_ in a _SUPERNOVA_.

new planetary nebula...   ...and a new solar system

Supernova

Neutron Star...

7) The _exploding supernova_ throws the outer layers of _dust and gas_ into space leaving a _very dense core_ called a _NEUTRON STAR_. If the star is _big enough_ this will become a _BLACK HOLE_.

...or Black Hole

8) The _dust and gas_ thrown off by the supernova will form into _SECOND GENERATION STARS_ like our Sun. The _heavier elements_ are _only_ made in the _final stages_ of a _big star_ just before the final _supernova_, so the _presence_ of heavier elements in the _Sun_ and the _inner planets_ is _clear evidence_ that our beautiful and wonderful world, with its warm sunsets and fresh morning dews, has all formed out of the snotty remains of a grisly old star's last dying sneeze.

9) The _matter_ from which _neutron stars_ and _white dwarfs_ and _black dwarfs_ are made is _MILLIONS OF TIMES DENSER_ than any matter on Earth because the _gravity is so strong_ it even crushes the _atoms_.

Twinkle Twinkle little star, How I wond.. — JUST LEARN IT PAL...

Erm. Just how do they know all that? As if it's not outrageous enough that they reckon to know the whole history of the Earth for the last five billion years, they also reckon to know the whole life cycle of stars, when they're all billions and billions of km away. It's just an outrage.

The Origin of the Universe

The _Big Bang Theory_ of the Universe is the most _convincing_ at the present time.
There is also the _steady state theory_ which is quite presentable but it _doesn't explain_ some of the observed features too well.

Red-shift needs Explaining

There are _TWO important bits of evidence_ you need to know about:

1) Light From Other Galaxies is Red-Shifted

1) When we look at _light_ from distant _galaxies_ we find that _all the frequencies_ are _shifted_ towards the _red end_ of the spectrum.
2) In other words the _frequencies_ are all _slightly lower_ than they should be. It's the same effect as a car _horn_ sounding lower-pitched when the car is travelling _away_ from you. The sound _drops in frequency_.
3) This is called the _Doppler effect_.
4) _Measurements_ of the red-shift suggest that _all_ the galaxies are _moving away from us_ very quickly — and it's the _same result_ whichever direction you look in.

2) The Further Away a Galaxy is , The Greater The Red-Shift

1) _More distant galaxies_ have _greater_ red-shifts than nearer ones.
2) This means that more distant galaxies are _moving away faster_ than nearer ones.
3) The _inescapable conclusion_ appears to be that the whole Universe is _expanding_.

The Big Bang Theory — Well Popular

1) Since all the galaxies appear to be _moving apart_ very rapidly, the obvious _conclusion_ is that there was an _initial explosion_: the _Big Bang_.
2) All the matter in the Universe must have been _compressed_ into a _very small space_ and then it _exploded_ and the _expansion_ is still going on.
3) The Big Bang is believed to have happened around _15 billion years ago_.
4) The age of the Universe can be _estimated_ from the current rate of _expansion_.
5) These estimates are _not very accurate_ because it's hard to tell how much the expansion has _slowed down_ since the Big Bang.
6) The rate at which the expansion is _slowing down_ is an _important factor_ in deciding the _future_ of the Universe.

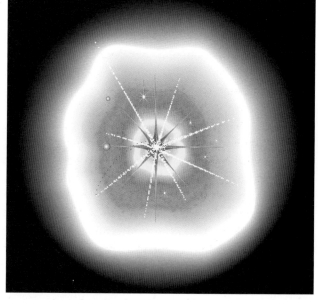

7) _Without gravity_ the Universe would expand at the _same rate forever_.
8) However, the _attraction_ between all the mass in the Universe tends to _slow_ the expansion down.

Red Shift — It's all in black and white before you...

The thing to learn here is the importance of _red shift_. Seven little points to _learn_, _cover_ and _jot down_, then on your lunch-break you can ponder the mysteries of the universe over sarnies.
You also need to know the important bits about the big bang theory and how it explains red shift.

Revision Summary for Module Eleven

More jolly questions which I know you're going to really enjoy. There are lots of bits and bobs on forces, motion and pressure which you definitely need to know. Some bits are certainly quite tricky to understand, but there's also loads of straightforward stuff which just need to be learnt, ready for instant regurgitation in the Exam. You have to practise these questions over and over and over again, until you can answer them all really easily — phew, such jolly fun.

1) Write down the formula for working out speed. Find the speed of a partly chewed mouse which hobbles 3.2m in 35s. Find how far he would get in 25 minutes.

2) What's acceleration? Is it the same thing as speed or velocity? What are the units of it?

3) Write down the formula for acceleration.
   What's the acceleration of a soggy pea, flicked from rest to a speed of 14 m/s in 0.4s?

4) Sketch a typical distance-time graph and point out all the important parts of it.

5) Sketch a typical velocity-time graph and point out all the important parts of it.

6) Explain how to calculate velocity from a distance-time graph.

7) Explain how to find speed, distance and acceleration from a velocity-time graph.

8) Write down the First Law of Motion. Illustrate with a diagram.

9) Write down the Second Law of Motion. Illustrate with a diagram. What's the formula for it?

10) A force of 30N pushes on a trolley of mass 4kg. What will be its acceleration?

11) What's the mass of a cat which accelerates at 9.8 m/s^2 when acted on by a force of 56N?

12) Write down the Third Law of Motion. Illustrate it with four diagrams.

13) Explain what reaction force is and where it pops up. Is it important to know about it?

14) What is gravity? List the three main effects that gravity produces.

15) What's the formula for weight? Illustrate it with a worked example of your own.

16) What is "terminal velocity"? Is it the same thing as maximum speed?

17) What are the two main factors affecting the terminal velocity of a falling object?

18) List the three types of friction with a sketch to illustrate each one.

19) What are the two different parts of the overall stopping distance of a car?

20) Calculate the Kinetic energy of a 78kg sheep running at a speed of 5m/s.

21) What's the formula for work done? A crazy dog drags a big branch 12m over the next-door neighbour's front lawn, pulling with a force of 535N. How much energy was transferred?

22) List the three or four factors which affect each of the two sections of stopping distance.

23) Sketch the important stretching springs graph and explain its shape. Explain "elastic" and "inelastic".

24) Sketch four diagrams showing how pressure is a) reduced and b) increased.

25) What happens to pressure as you go deeper? Which direction does the pressure act in?

26) What's the formula for pressure? What units is pressure given in? What's the definition?

27) Sketch a jack and a car braking system and explain how they work as force multipliers.

28) What is the pressure law ? Sketch an experiment which demonstrates it. What's the formula?

29) A fixed amount of gas at 5,000 Pa is compressed down to 60cm^3, and in the process its pressure rises to 260,000 Pa. What was the volume before it got compressed?

30) Which parts of the world have the longest days and which parts have the shortest days?

31) List the eleven parts of the Solar System starting with the Sun, and get them in the right order.

32) How does the Sun produce all its heat? What does the Sun give out?

33) What is it that keeps the planets in their orbits? What other things are held in orbits?

34) What are constellations? What do planets do in the constellations?

35) Explain fully what a geostationary satellite does, and state what they're used for.

36) Explain fully what a low polar orbit satellite does, and state what they're used for.

37) Which of the two types of satellite takes longer to orbit the Earth? Explain why.

38) What do stars and solar systems form from? What force causes it all to happen?

39) What is the Milky Way? Sketch it and show our Sun in relation to it.

40) Describe the first stages of a star's formation. Where does the initial energy come from?

41) What process eventually starts inside the star to make it produce so much heat and light?

42) What are the final two stages of: a) a small star's life? b) a big star's life?

43) What is the main theory for the origin of the Universe? Give brief details of the theory.

44) What are the two important bits of evidence which need explaining by this theory?

Waves — Basic Principles

Waves are different from anything else. They have various features which _only waves have_:

Amplitude, Wavelength and Frequency

Too many people get these _wrong_. Take careful note:

1) The _AMPLITUDE_ goes from the _middle_ line to the _peak_, NOT from a trough to a peak.
2) The _WAVELENGTH_ covers a _full cycle_ of the wave, e.g. from _peak to peak_, not just from "_two bits that are sort of separated a bit_".
3) _FREQUENCY_ is how many _complete waves_ there are _per second_ (passing a certain point).

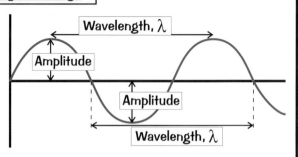

Transverse Waves have Sideways Vibrations

Most waves are _TRANSVERSE_:

1) _Light_ and all other _EM radiation_.
2) _Ripples_ on water.
3) _Waves_ on _strings_.
4) A _slinky spring_ wiggled up and down.

In _TRANSVERSE WAVES_ the vibrations are at _90⁰_ to the _direction of travel_ of the wave.

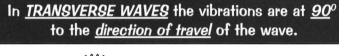

Vibrations from side to side | Wave travelling this way

Longitudinal Waves have Vibrations along the Same Line

The ONLY longitudinal waves are:

1) _Sound_. It travels as a longitudinal wave through solids, liquids and gases.
2) _Shock waves_ e.g. seismic _P-waves_.
3) A _slinky spring_ when plucked.
4) _Don't get confused_ by CRO displays which shows a _transverse wave_ when displaying _sounds_. The real wave is _longitudinal_ — the display shows a transverse wave _just so you can see what's going on_.

In _LONGITUDINAL WAVES_ the vibrations are _ALONG THE SAME DIRECTION_ as the wave is travelling.

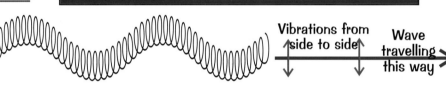

One wavelength | Rarefactions | Compressions

Vibrations in same direction as wave is travelling

All Waves Carry Energy — Without Transferring Matter

1) _Light_, _infrared_, and _microwaves_ all make things _warm up_. _X-rays_ and _gamma rays_ can cause _ionisation_ and _damage_ to cells, which also shows that they carry _energy_.
2) _Loud_ sounds make things _vibrate or move_. Even the quietest sound moves your _ear drum_.
3) Waves on the sea can _toss big boats around_ and can generate _electricity_.

Waves can be REFLECTED and REFRACTED and DIFFRACTED

1) They might test whether or not you realise these are _properties_ of waves, so _learn them_.
2) The three words are _confusingly similar_ but you _MUST_ learn the _differences_ between them.
3) Light and sound are _reflected_, _refracted_ and _diffracted_ and this shows they travel as waves.

Learn about waves — just get into the vibes, man...

This is all very basic stuff on waves. Five sections with some tasty titbits in each. _Learn_ the headings, then the details. Then _cover the page_ and see what you can _scribble down_. Then try again until you can remember the whole lot. It's all just _easy marks to be won... or lost_.

Reflection

They're just formulae, *just like all the other formulae*, and the *same old rules apply*.
Mind you, there's a few *extra details* that go with these wave formulae. Learn them now:

The First Rule: Try and Choose the Right Formula

1) People have *way too much difficulty* deciding which *formula* to use.

2) All too often the question starts with "*A wave is travelling...*", and in they leap with "v = fλ".

3) To choose the *right formula* you have to look for the *THREE quantities* mentioned in the question.

4) If the question mentions *speed*, *frequency* and *wavelength* then sure, "v = fλ" is the one to use.

5) But if it has *speed*, *time* and *distance* then "s = d/t" is more the order of the day — *wouldn't you say*.

Example — Water Ripples

a) *Some ripples travel 55cm in 5 seconds. Find their speed in cm/s.*
   ANSWER: Speed, distance and time are mentioned in the question,
       so we must use "s=d/t": s = d/t = 55/5 = **11 cm/s**

b) *The wavelength of these waves is found to be 2.2cm. What is their frequency?*
   ANSWER: This time we have f and λ mentioned, so we use "v = fλ", and we'll need this:
   which tells us that f = v/λ = 11cm/s ÷ 2.2cm = **5Hz** *(It's very cool to use cm/s with cm, s and Hz)*

The Ripple Tank is Really Good for Displaying Waves

Learn all these diagrams showing *reflection of waves*. They could ask you to complete *any one of them* in the Exam. It can be quite a bit *trickier* than you think unless you've *practised* them real well *beforehand*.

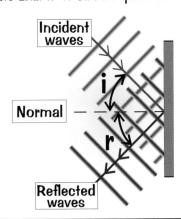

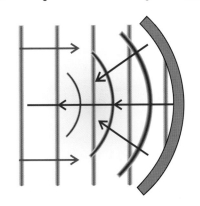

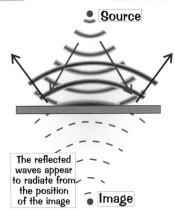

Source

The reflected waves appear to radiate from the position of the image • Image

---

Reflection of Light

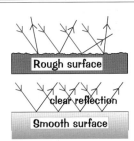

Reflection of light is what allows us to *SEE* objects.
When light reflects from an *even* surface (*smooth and shiny* like a *mirror*) then it's all reflected at the *same angle* and you get a *clear reflection*.
Sound also reflects off *hard surfaces* in the form of *echoes*.
Reflection of light and of sound gives evidence that light and sound travel as waves.
And don't forget, *THE LAW OF REFLECTION* applies to *every reflected ray*:

Rough surface

clear reflection

Smooth surface

Angle of <u>INCIDENCE</u> = Angle of <u>REFLECTION</u>

Learn reflection thoroughly — try to look at it from all sides...

First make sure you can draw all those diagrams from memory. Then make sure you've learnt the rest well enough to answer typical meany Exam questions like these: *"Explain why you can see a piece of paper"* *"Why is the image in a plane mirror virtual?"*

Refraction

1) _Refraction_ is when waves change _direction_ as they enter a _different medium_.
2) This is caused _entirely_ by the _change in speed_ of the waves.
3) It also causes the _wavelength_ to change, but remember that the _frequency_ does _not_ change.

1) Refraction is Shown by Waves in a Ripple Tank Slowing Down

1) The waves travel _slower_ in _shallower water_, causing _refraction_ as shown.
2) There's a change in _direction_, and a change in _wavelength_ but _NO change_ in _frequency_.

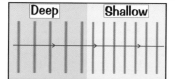
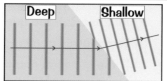

2) Refraction of Light — The Good Old Glass Block Demo

You can't fail to remember the old _"ray of light through a rectangular glass block"_ trick. Make sure you can draw this diagram _from memory_, with every detail _perfect_.

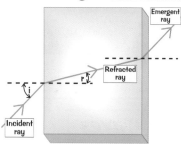

1) _Take careful note_ of the positions of the _normals_ and the _exact positions_ of the angles of _incidence_ and _refraction_ (and note it's the angle of _refraction_ — not _reflection_).
2) Most important of all remember _which way_ the ray _bends_ — _towards_ the normal as it enters the _denser medium_, _away_ from the normal as it emerges into the _less dense_ medium.
3) Try to _visualise_ the shape of the _wiggle_ in the diagram — that can be easier than remembering the rule in words.

3) Refraction Is always Caused By the Waves Changing Speed

1) When waves _slow down_ they bend _towards_ the normal.
2) When _light_ enters _glass_ it _slows down_ to about _2/3_ of its speed in air.
3) When waves hit the boundary _along a normal_, i.e. at _exactly 90°_, then there will be _no change_ in direction — this is _important_. There'll still be a change in _speed_ and _wavelength_, though.
4) _Some_ light is also _reflected_ when light hits a _different medium_ such as glass.
5) _Sound_ refracts too...

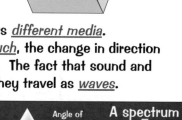

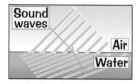

Sound will also refract (change direction) as it enters _different media_. However, since sound is always _spreading out so much_, the change in direction is _hard to spot_. Just remember, _sound does refract_. The fact that sound and light are both refracted gives _further evidence_ that they travel as _waves_.

4) Dispersion Produces Rainbows

1) _Different colours_ of light are _refracted_ by _different amounts_. This is because they travel at _slightly different speeds_ in any given _medium_.
2) If white light enters a _prism_, each different colour in it emerges at a _different angle_, producing a _spectrum_ of the rainbow colours. This effect is known as _DISPERSION_.
3) You will need to remember the order of the colours   Red Orange Yellow Green Blue Indigo Violet and this can be done by learning the following....   Richard Of York Gave Battle In Vain
4) You need to know that _red light_ is refracted the _least_ — and _violet_ is refracted the _most_. Also learn where _infrared_ and _ultraviolet_ light would appear if you could detect them.

Revise Refraction — but don't let it slow you down...

The first thing you've gotta do is make sure you can spot the difference between the words _refraction_ and _reflection_. After that you need to _learn all this stuff about refraction_ — so you know exactly what it is. Make sure you know all those _diagrams_ inside out. _Cover and scribble._

Refraction: Two Special Cases

Total Internal Reflection and The Critical Angle

1) This _only_ happens when _light_ is _coming out_ of something _dense_ like _glass_ or _water_ or _perspex_.
2) If the _angle_ is _shallow enough_ the ray _won't come out at all_, but it _reflects_ back into the glass
   (or whatever).   This is called _total internal reflection_ because __ALL__ of the light _reflects back in_.
3) You definitely need to learn this set of __THREE DIAGRAMS__ which show the three conditions:

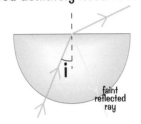

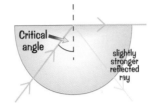

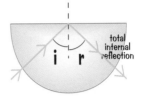

Angle of Incidence LESS than
the Critical Angle.
Most of the light _passes through_
into the air but a _little_ bit of it is
internally reflected.

Angle of Incidence EQUAL TO
the Critical Angle.
The emerging ray comes out _along_
the surface. There's quite a bit of
internal reflection.

Angle of Incidence GREATER
than the Critical Angle.
No light comes out.
It's _all_ internally reflected,
i.e. _total internal reflection_.

1) The _Critical Angle_ for _glass_ is about 42°. This is _very handy_ because it means _45° angles_ can be used
   to get _total internal reflection_ as in the _prisms_ in the _periscope_ shown below.
2) In __DIAMOND__ the _Critical Angle_ is much _lower_, about 24°. This is the reason why diamonds _sparkle_ so
   much, because there are lots of _internal reflections_.

Periscope

Periscopes use _Total Internal Reflection_ of light in _45° prisms_.
Prisms are used because they give a slightly _better reflection_ than
a _mirror_ would and they're also _easier_ to hold accurately _in place_.
They could ask you to _complete_ a diagram of a periscope and unless you've
practised beforehand you'll find it _pretty tricky_ to draw the prisms in _properly_.

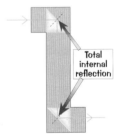

Total internal reflection

Optical Fibres — Communications and Endoscopes

1) _Optical fibres_ can carry _information_ over _long distances_ by repeated _total internal reflections_.
2) Optical communications have several _advantages_ over _electrical signals_ in wires:
   a) a cable of the _same diameter_ can carry a lot _more information_.
   b) the signals cannot be _tapped into_, or suffer _interference_ from electrical sources.
   c) the signal doesn't need _boosting_ as often.
3) The fibre must be _narrow enough_ to
   keep the angles _above_ the critical
   angle, as shown, so the fibre mustn't
   be bent _too sharply_ anywhere.

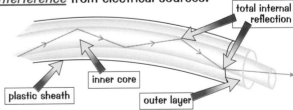

total internal reflection

inner core

plastic sheath

outer layer

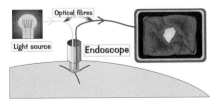

An endoscope is a _narrow bunch_ of _optical fibres_ with a _lens system_ at
each end. Another bunch of fibres carries light down _inside_ to see with.
The image is displayed as a _full colour moving image_ on a TV screen.
This means they can do operations _without_ cutting big holes in people.

Total Internal Reflection — sounds like a Government Inquiry...

Three sections to learn here, with diagrams for each. They always have _at least one_ of these
applications of total internal reflection in the Exam. _Learn them all_. None of this is difficult —
but just make sure you've got all those little picky details firmly fastened inside your head.

Diffraction

This word sounds a lot more technical than it really is.

Diffraction is Just the "Spreading Out" of Waves

All waves tend to *spread out* at the *edges* when they pass through a *gap* or *past an object*. Instead of saying that the wave *"spreads out"* or *"bends"* round a corner you should say that it *DIFFRACTS* around the corner. It's as easy as that. That's all diffraction means.

A Wave Spreads More if it Passes Through a Narrow Gap

The *ripple tank* shows this effect quite nicely. The same effect applies to *light* and *sound* too.

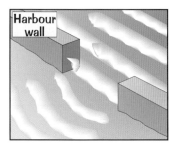

1) A *"narrow"* gap is one which is about the *same size* as the *wavelength* or *less*.
2) Obviously then, the question of whether a gap is *"narrow"* or not depends on the *wave* in question. What may be a *narrow* gap for a *water* wave will be a *huge* gap for a *light* wave.
3) It should be obvious then, that the *longer* the wavelength of a wave *the more it will diffract*.

Sounds Always Diffract Quite a Lot, Because λ is Quite Big

1) Most sounds have wavelengths *in air* of around *0.1m*, which is quite long.
2) This means they *spread out round corners* so you can still *hear* people even when you can't *see* them directly (the sound usually *reflects* off walls too which also helps).
3) *Higher frequency sounds* will have *shorter wavelengths* and so they won't diffract as much, which is why things sound more *"muffled"* when you hear them from round corners.

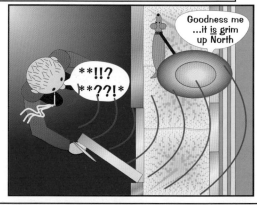

Long Wavelength Radio Waves Diffract Easily Over Hills and into Buildings:

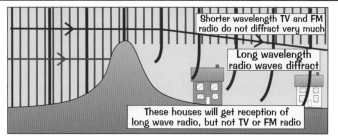

Shorter wavelength TV and FM radio do not diffract very much

Long wavelength radio waves diffract

These houses will get reception of long wave radio, but not TV or FM radio

Visible Light on the other hand...

has a *very short wavelength*, and it'll only diffract with a *very narrow slit*:

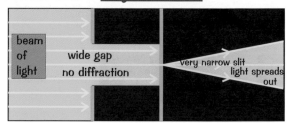

beam of light
wide gap no diffraction
very narrow slit light spreads out

This spreading or *diffraction* of light (and radio waves) is *strong evidence* for the *wave nature of light*.

Diffraction — it can drive you round the bend...

People usually don't know much about diffraction, mainly because there are so few lab demos you can do to show it, and there's also very little to say about it — about one page's worth, in fact. The thing is though, if you just *learn this page properly*, then you'll *know all you need to*.

The EM Spectrum

The Electromagnetic Spectrum

There are Seven Basic Types of Electromagnetic Wave

We split Electromagnetic waves (EM waves) into _seven_ basic types as shown below.
These EM waves form a _continuous spectrum_ so the different regions do actually _merge_ into each other.

RADIO WAVES	MICRO WAVES	INFRA RED	VISIBLE LIGHT	ULTRA VIOLET	X-RAYS	GAMMA RAYS
$1m - 10^4 m$	$10^{-2} m$ (3cm)	$10^{-5} m$ (0.01mm)	$10^{-7} m$	$10^{-8} m$	$10^{-10} m$	$10^{-12} m$

Our _eyes_ can only detect a _very narrow range_ of EM waves which are the ones we call (visible) _light_.
All EM waves travel at _exactly_ the same _speed_ as light in a _vacuum_, and _pretty much_ the same speed
as light in _other media_ like glass or water — though this is always _slower_ than their speed in vacuum.

As the Wavelength Changes, So Do The Properties

1) As the _wavelength_ of EM radiation changes, its _interaction_ with matter changes. In particular the way
   any EM wave is _absorbed_, _reflected_ or _transmitted_ by any given substance depends _entirely_ on its
   wavelength — that's the whole point of these three pages of course!
2) When _any_ EM radiation is _absorbed_ it can cause _two effects_:
       a) _Heating_   b) Creation of a _tiny alternating current_ with the _same_ frequency as the radiation.
3) You need to know all the details that follow about all the different parts of the EM spectrum:

Radio Waves are Used Mainly For Communications

1) _Radio Waves_ are used mainly for _communication_.
2) Both _TV and FM Radio_ use _short wavelength_ radio waves of about
   Im wavelength.
3) To receive these wavelengths you need to be more or less in _direct
   sight_ of the transmitter, because they will _not_ bend (diffract) over
   hills or travel very far _through_ buildings.
4) The _longer wavelengths_ can travel further because they are

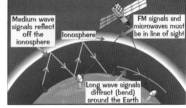

   reflected from an _electrically charged layer_ in the Earth's upper atmosphere (the ionosphere).
   This means they can be sent further around the Earth.

Microwaves Are Used For Cooking and Satellite Signals

1) _Microwaves_ have _two_ main uses:
   cooking food and _satellite_ transmissions.
2) Satellite transmissions use a frequency of microwaves
   which _passes easily_ through the _Earth's atmosphere_,
   including _clouds_, which seems pretty sensible.

3) The frequency used for _cooking_, on the other hand is one which is readily _absorbed_ by _water
   molecules_. The microwaves pass easily _into the food_ and are then _absorbed_ by the _water molecules_
   and turn into heat _inside_ the food.
4) Microwaves can therefore be _dangerous_ because they can be absorbed by _living tissue_ and the heat
   will _damage or kill_ the cells causing a sort of _"cold burn"_.

The spectrum — isn't that something kinda rude in Biology...

There are lots of details on this page that you definitely need to know. The top diagram is an
absolute must — they usually give it you with one or two missing labels to be filled in. _Learn_
the four sections on this page then _scribble_ a _mini-essay_ for each one to see what you know.

The EM Spectrum

Visible light is Used To See With and In Optical Fibres

Visible Light is pretty useful. It's used in _Optical Fibre Digital Communications_ and endoscopes which are the best ones for your answer _in the Exam_ (see P.93).

Infrared Radiation — Toasters and Remote Controls

1) _Infrared_ (or IR) is otherwise known as _heat radiation_. This is given out by all _hot objects_ and you _feel it_ on your _skin_ as _radiant heat_. Infrared is readily _absorbed_ by _all_ materials and _causes heating_.

2) _Radiant heaters_ (i.e. those that _glow red_) use infrared radiation, including _toasters_ and _grills_.

3) _Over-exposure_ to infrared causes _damage_ to cells. This is what causes _sunburn_.

4) Infrared is also used for all the _remote controls_ of _TV's and videos_.

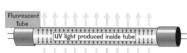

Ultraviolet Light Causes Skin Cancer

1) This is what causes _skin cancer_ if you spend _too much time_ in the _sun_.

2) It also causes your skin to _tan_. _Sunbeds_ give out UV rays but _less harmful ones_ than the Sun does.

3) _Darker skin_ protects against UV rays by _preventing_ them from reaching more vulnerable _skin tissues_ deeper down.

4) There are special _coatings_ which _absorb_ UV light and then _give out visible light_ instead. These are used to coat the inside of _fluorescent tubes_ and lamps.

5) Ultra violet is also useful for hidden _security marks_ which are written in special ink that can only be seen with an ultraviolet light.

X-Rays Are Used in Hospitals, but are Pretty Dangerous

1) These are used in _hospitals_ to take _X-ray photographs_ of people to see whether they have any _broken bones_.

2) X-rays pass easily through _flesh_ but not through _denser material_ such as _bones_ or _metal_.

3) X-rays can cause _cancer_, so _radiographers_, who take X-ray pictures _all day long_ wear _lead aprons_ and stand behind a _lead screen_ to keep their _exposure_ to X-rays to a _minimum_.

Gamma Rays Cause Cancer but Are Used to Treat it Too

1) Gamma Rays are used to kill _harmful bacteria_ in food to keep it _fresher for longer_.

2) They are also used to _sterilise medical instruments_, again by _killing the bacteria_.

3) They can also be used in the _treatment of cancer_ because they _kill cancer cells_.

4) Gamma rays tend to _pass through_ soft tissue but _some_ are _absorbed_ by the cells.

5) In _high doses_, Gamma rays (along with X-rays and UV rays) can _kill normal cells_.

6) In _lower doses_ all these three types of EM Waves can cause normal cells to become _cancerous_.

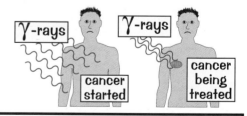

Radiographers are like Teachers — they can see right through you...

Here are the other five parts of the EM spectrum for you to learn. Ace, isn't it. At least there's some groovy diagrams to help relieve the tedium. On this page there are five sections.

Do a _mini-essay_ for each section, then _check_, _re-learn_, _re-scribble_, _re-check_, etc. etc.

Sound Waves

1) Sound travels as a wave:

Sound can be _reflected_ off walls (echoes), it can be _refracted_ as it passes into different media and it can _diffract_ around doors. These are all standard properties of waves so we deduce that _sound travels as a wave_. This "sound" reasoning can also be applied to deduce the wave nature of light.

2) The Frequency of a Sound Wave Determines its Pitch

1) _High frequency sound waves_ sound _HIGH PITCHED_ like a _squeaking mouse_.
2) _Low frequency_ sound waves sound _LOW PITCHED_ like a _mooing cow_.
3) _Frequency_ is the number of complete _vibrations_ each second. It's measured in _Hertz_, _Hz_.
4) Other common units are _kHz_ (1000 Hz) and _MHz_ (1,000,000 Hz).
5) _High frequency_ (or high pitch) also means _shorter wavelength_.
6) The range of frequencies heard by humans is from 20Hz to 20kHz.
7) These _CRO screens_ are _very important_ so make sure you know all about them:

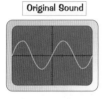
Original Sound

The CRO screens tell us about the _pitch_ and _loudness_ of the sound:

Lower pitched

2) When the peaks are _further apart_ then the sound is at a _lower pitch_ (a lower frequency).

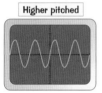
Higher pitched

1) The _closer_ the peaks are together, the _higher_ pitched the sound (and the _higher_ the frequency).

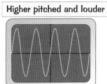
Higher pitched and louder

3) The CRO screen will show _large peaks_ for a _loud noise_ (sound waves with a _big amplitude_).

3) Amplitude is a Measure of the Energy Carried by Any Wave

1) The greater the _AMPLITUDE_, the _more ENERGY_ the wave carries.
2) In _SOUND_ this means it'll be _LOUDER_.
3) _Bigger amplitude_ means a _louder sound_.
4) With _LIGHT_, a bigger amplitude means it'll be _BRIGHTER_.

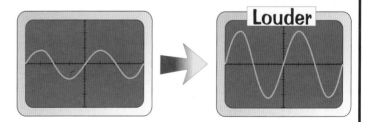
Louder

4) Echoes and Reverberation are due to REFLECTED Sound

1) Sound will only be _reflected_ from _hard flat surfaces_. Things like _carpets_ and _curtains_ act as _absorbing surfaces_ which will _absorb_ sounds rather than reflect them.
2) This is very noticeable in the _reverberation_ in an _empty room_. A big empty room sounds _completely different_ once you've put carpet and curtains in, and a bit of furniture, because these things absorb the sound quickly and stop it _echoing_ (reverberating) around the room.

If sound travelled through vacuum — sunny days would be deafening...

Once again the page is broken up into five sections with important numbered points for each. All those numbered points are important. They're all mentioned specifically in the syllabuses so you should expect them to test exactly this stuff in the Exams. _Learn and enjoy._

Ultrasound

Ultrasound is Sound with a Higher Frequency than We Can Hear

Electrical devices can be made which produce *electrical oscillations* of *any frequency*. These can easily be converted into *mechanical vibrations* to produce *sound* waves *beyond the range of human hearing* (i.e. frequencies above 20kHz). This is called **ULTRASOUND** and it has loads of uses:

1) Industrial Cleaning

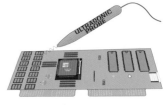

ULTRASOUND CAN BE USED TO CLEAN DELICATE MECHANISMS without them having to be *dismantled*. The ultrasound waves can be directed on *very precise areas* and are extremely effective at *removing dirt* and other deposits which form on *delicate equipment*. The alternatives would either *damage* the equipment or else would require it to be *dismantled* first.
THE SAME TECHNIQUE IS USED FOR CLEANING TEETH.
Dentists use *ultrasonic tools* to easily and *painlessly* remove hard deposits of *tartar* which build up on teeth and which would lead to *gum disease*.

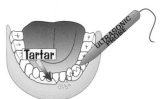

2) Industrial Quality Control

Ultrasound waves can pass through something like a *metal casting* and whenever they reach a *boundary* between *two different media* (like metal and air) some of the wave is *reflected back* and *detected*. The exact *timing and distribution* of these *echoes* give *detailed information* about the *internal structure*.
The echoes are usually *processed by computer* to produce a *visual display* of what the object must be like *inside*.
If there are cracks where there shouldn't be *they'll show up*.

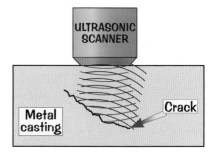

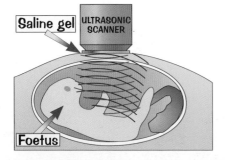

3) For Pre-Natal Scanning of a Foetus

This follows the *same principle* as the industrial quality control. As the ultrasound hits *different media* some of the sound wave is *reflected* and these reflected waves are *processed by computer* to produce a *video image* of the foetus. Ultrasound waves are *completely harmless* to the foetus, *unlike X-rays* which would be very dangerous.

4) Range and Direction Finding — SONAR

Bats send out *high-pitched squeaks* (ultrasound) and pick up the *reflections* with their *big ears*. Their brains are able to *process* the reflected signal and turn it into a *picture* of what's around.
So the bats basically "*see*" with *sound waves*, well enough in fact to *catch moths* in *mid-flight* in *complete darkness* — it's a nice trick if you can do it.
The same technique is used for *SONAR* which uses *sound waves underwater* to detect features on the sea-bed. The *pattern* of the reflections indicates the *depth* and basic features.

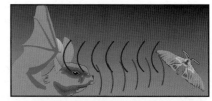

Ultrasound — weren't they a pop group...

Geesh — two pages on sound and with eight sections in total. No numbered points this time though. That means the mini-essay method is going to be a better idea. *Learn* the eight headings, then *cover the pages* and *scribble a mini-essay* for each, with diagrams. Enjoy.

Seismic Waves

Seismic Waves Are Caused By Earthquakes

1) We can only drill _about 10km_ or so into the crust of the Earth, which is not very far, so _seismic waves_ are really the _only_ way of investigating the _inner structure_.
2) When there's an _Earthquake_ somewhere the _shock waves_ travel out from it and we _detect_ them all over the surface of the planet using _seismographs_.
3) We measure the _time_ it takes for the _two different types_ of shock wave to reach each _seismograph_.
4) We also note the parts of the Earth which _don't receive the shock waves_ at all.
5) From this information you can work out _all sorts of stuff_ about the inside of the Earth as shown below:

S-Waves and P-Waves Take Different Paths

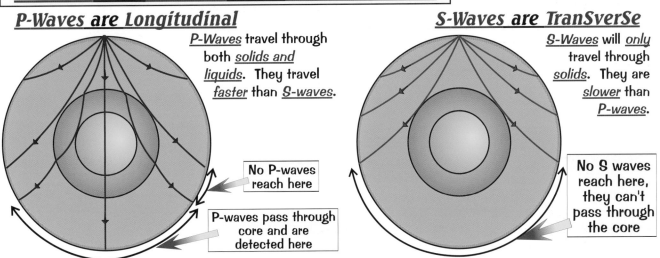

P-Waves are Longitudinal

P-Waves travel through both _solids and liquids_. They travel _faster_ than _S-waves_.

No P-waves reach here

P-waves pass through core and are detected here

S-Waves are TranSverSe

S-Waves will _only_ travel through _solids_. They are _slower_ than _P-waves_.

No S waves reach here, they can't pass through the core

The Seismograph Results Tell Us What's Down There

1) About _halfway_ through the Earth, there's an abrupt _change in direction_ of both types of wave. This indicates that there's a sudden _increase in density_ at that point — the _CORE_.
2) The fact that S-waves are _not_ detected in the _shadow_ of this core tells us that it's very _liquid_.
3) It's also found that _P-waves_ travel _slightly faster_ through the _middle_ of the core, which strongly suggests that there's a _solid inner core_.
4) Note that _S-waves_ do travel through the _mantle_ which suggests that it's kinda _solid_, though I always thought it was made of _molten lava_ which looks pretty _liquidy_ to me when it comes _sploshing_ out of volcanoes. Still there you go, just another one of life's little conundrums, I guess.

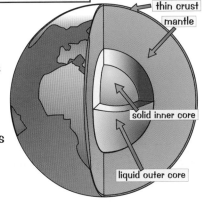

thin crust
mantle
solid inner core
liquid outer core

The Paths Curve Due to Increasing Density (causing Refraction)

1) Both _S-waves_ and _P-waves_ travel _faster_ in _more dense_ material.
2) The _curvature_ of their paths is due to the _increasing density_ of the _mantle_ and _core_ with depth.
3) When the density changes _suddenly_, the waves change direction _abruptly_, as shown above.
4) The paths _curve_ because the density of both the mantle and the core _increases steadily_ with increasing depth. The waves _gradually change direction_ because their speed is _gradually changing_, due to gradual changes in the _density_ of the medium. This is _refraction_, of course.

Seismic Waves — they reveal the terrible trembling truth...

The last page on waves. Hoorah. Once again there are four main sections to learn. _Learn_ the headings first, then try _scribbling down_ all the details for each heading, including the diagrams. Remember that S-waves are tranSverSe — so P-waves must be the longitudinal ones.

Types of Radiation

Don't get _mixed up_ between _nuclear_ radiation which is _dangerous_ — and _electromagnetic_ radiation which _generally isn't_. Gamma radiation is included in both, of course.

A substance which gives out radiation all the time is called _radioactive_.

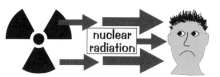
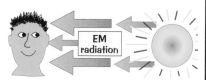

Nuclear Radiation: Alpha, Beta and Gamma (α, β and γ)

You need to remember _three things_ about _each type of radiation_:
1) What they actually _are_.
2) How well they _penetrate_ materials.
3) How strongly they _ionise_ that material. (_i.e._ bash into atoms and _knock electrons off_)
   There's a pattern — the _further_ the radiation can _penetrate_ before hitting an atom and getting stopped, the _less damage_ it will do along the way and so the _less ionising_ it is.

Alpha Particles are Helium Nuclei

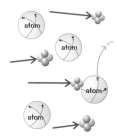

1) They are relatively _big_ and _heavy_ and _slow moving_.
2) They therefore _don't_ penetrate into materials but are _stopped quickly_.
3) Because of their size they are _strongly_ ionising, which just means they _bash into_ a lot of atoms and _knock electrons off_ them before they slow down, which creates lots of ions — hence the term "_ionising_".

Beta Particles are Electrons

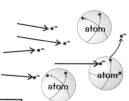

1) These are _in between_ alpha and gamma in terms of their _properties_.
2) They move _quite_ fast and they are _quite_ small (they're electrons).
3) They _penetrate moderately_ before colliding and are _moderately ionising_ too.
4) For every _β–particle_ emitted, a _neutron_ turns to a _proton_ in the nucleus.

Gamma Rays are Very Short Wavelength EM Waves

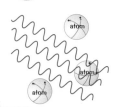

1) They are the _opposite_ of alpha particles in a way.
2) They _penetrate a long way_ into materials without being stopped.
3) This means they are _weakly_ ionising because they tend to _pass through_ rather than colliding with atoms. Eventually they _hit something_ and do _damage_.

Remember What Blocks the Three Types of Radiation...

As radiation _passes through_ materials some of the radiation is _absorbed_. The greater the _thickness_ of material the _more absorption_ occurs.

They really like this for Exam questions, so make sure _you know_ what it takes to _block_ each of the _three_:

  ALPHA particles are blocked by _paper_.
  BETA particles are blocked by thin _aluminium_.
  GAMMA rays are blocked by _thick lead_.

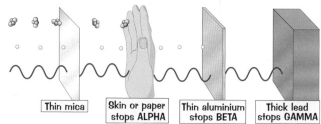

Thin mica | Skin or paper stops ALPHA | Thin aluminium stops BETA | Thick lead stops GAMMA

Of course anything _equivalent_ will also block them, e.g. _skin_ will stop _alpha_, but _not_ the others; a thin sheet of _any metal_ will stop _beta_; and _very thick concrete_ will stop _gamma_ just like lead does.

Learn the three types of radiation — it's easy as abc...

Alpha, beta and gamma. You do realise those are just the first three letters of the Greek alphabet don't you: α, β, γ — just like a, b, c. They might sound like complex names to you but they were just easy labels at the time. Anyway, _learn all the facts_ about them — and _scribble_.

Background Radiation

Background Radiation Comes From Many Sources

Natural background radiation comes from:

1) Radioactivity of naturally occurring <u>unstable isotopes</u> which are <u>all around us</u> — in the <u>air</u>, in <u>food</u>, in <u>building materials</u> and in the <u>rocks</u> under our feet.
2) Radiation from <u>space</u>, which is known as <u>cosmic rays</u>. These come mostly from the <u>Sun</u>.
3) Radiation due to <u>human activity</u>. i.e. <u>fallout</u> from <u>nuclear explosions</u> or <u>dumped nuclear waste</u>. But this represents a <u>tiny</u> proportion of the total background radiation.

The RELATIVE PROPORTIONS of *background radiation*:

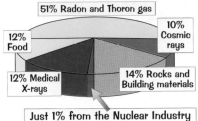

- 51% Radon and Thoron gas
- 10% Cosmic rays
- 12% Food
- 12% Medical X-rays
- 14% Rocks and Building materials
- Just 1% from the Nuclear Industry

The <u>level</u> of <u>background radiation</u> changes, depending on <u>where you are</u>:

1) At <u>high altitudes</u> (e.g. in <u>jet planes</u>) it <u>increases</u> because of more exposure to <u>cosmic rays</u>.

Coloured bits indicate more radiation from rocks

2) <u>Underground in mines</u>, etc. it increases because of the <u>rocks</u> all around. Rocks like <u>granite</u> have a high background count.
3) Certain <u>underground rocks</u> can cause higher levels at the <u>surface</u>, especially if they release <u>radioactive radon gas</u>, which tends to get trapped <u>inside people's houses</u>. This varies widely across the UK depending on the <u>rock type</u>, as shown.

Radiation Harms Living Cells

1) <u>Alpha</u>, <u>beta</u> and <u>gamma</u> radiation will cheerfully enter living cells and <u>collide</u> with molecules.
2) These collisions cause <u>ionisation</u>, which <u>damages</u> or <u>destroys</u> the molecules.
3) <u>Lower</u> doses tend to cause <u>minor</u> damage without <u>killing</u> the cell.
4) This can give rise to <u>mutant</u> cells which divide <u>uncontrollably</u>. This is <u>cancer</u>.
5) <u>Higher</u> doses tend to <u>kill cells</u> completely, which causes <u>radiation sickness</u> if a lot of your body cells <u>all get blatted at once</u>.
6) The <u>extent</u> of the harmful effects depends on <u>two things</u>:
   a) How much <u>exposure</u> you have to the radiation.
   b) The <u>energy</u> and <u>penetration</u> of the radiation emitted, since some types are <u>more hazardous</u> than others, of course.

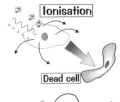
Ionisation / Dead cell

radiation hits nucleus / damaged cell / cancer

Outside The Body, β– and γ–Sources are the Most Dangerous

This is because <u>beta and gamma</u> can get <u>inside</u> to the delicate <u>organs</u>, whereas alpha is much less dangerous because it <u>can't penetrate</u> the skin.

Inside The Body, an α–Source is the Most Dangerous

<u>Inside the body</u> alpha-sources do all their damage in a <u>very localised area</u>. Beta and gamma sources on the other hand are <u>less dangerous</u> inside the body because they mostly <u>pass straight out</u> without doing much damage.

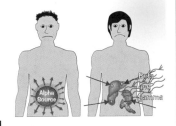
Alpha Source / Beta and Gamma

Radiotherapy — the Treatment of Cancer Using γ-Rays

Since high doses of gamma rays will <u>kill all living cells</u> they can be used to <u>treat cancers</u>. The gamma rays have to be directed <u>carefully</u> and at just the right <u>dosage</u> so as to kill the <u>cancer cells</u> without damaging too many <u>normal cells</u>.

Background Radiation — it's no good burying your head in the sand...

Yip, it's funny old stuff is radiation, that's for sure. It is quite mysterious, I guess, but just like anything else, the <u>more you learn about it</u>, the <u>less</u> of a mystery it becomes. This page is positively bristling with simple straightforward facts about radiation. Some tiny little <u>mini-essays</u> practised two or three times and all this knowledge will be yours — forever. Enjoy. ☺

Uses of Radioactive Materials

This is a nice _easy bit_ of straightforward learning. Below are _three uses_ for radioactive isotopes. Make sure you _learn all_ the details. In particular, make sure you get the grip of why each application uses a _particular radio-isotope_ according to its _half-life_ and the _type of radiation_ it gives out.

1) Tracers in Medicine — always Short Half-life γ-emitters

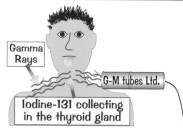

Gamma Rays

G-M tubes Ltd.

Iodine-131 collecting in the thyroid gland

1) Certain _radioactive isotopes_ can be _injected_ into or swallowed by people, and their progress _around the body_ can be monitored using a _detector_, whose signal can be converted to a _TV display_ showing where the _strongest_ reading is coming from. A well known example is the use of _Iodine-131_ which is absorbed by the _thyroid gland_, just like normal Iodine-127, but it gives out _radiation_ which can be _detected_ to indicate whether or not the thyroid gland is _taking in the iodine_ as it should.

2) _All isotopes_ which are taken _into the body_ must _always_ be _GAMMA sources_, (never alpha or beta), so that the radiation _passes out_ of the body and they must also have a _short_ half-life of just _a few hours_, so that the radioactivity inside the patient _quickly_ disappears.

2) Tracers in Industry — For Finding Leaks

This is _much the same technique_ as the medical tracers.

1) Radio-isotopes can be used to detect _leaks_ in pipes. Just add the radio-isotope to the liquid and use a _detector_ to find the areas along the pipe where radioactivity is _high_, which is where the leaks are.

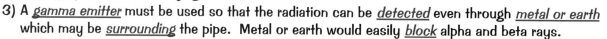

G-M tubes Ltd.

2) This is really useful for _concealed_ or _underground_ pipes, to save you digging up half the road trying to find the leak.

3) A _gamma emitter_ must be used so that the radiation can be _detected_ even through _metal or earth_ which may be _surrounding_ the pipe. Metal or earth would easily _block_ alpha and beta rays.

4) It should also have a _short half-life_ so as not to cause a _hazard_ if it collects somewhere.

3) Thickness Control in Industry and Manufacturing

1) You have a _radioactive source_ and you direct it _through_ the stuff being made, usually a continuous sheet of _paper_ or _cardboard_ or _metal_ etc.

2) The _detector_ is on the _other side_ and is connected to a _control unit_.

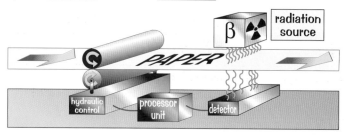

β radiation source

PAPER

hydraulic control

processor unit

detector

3) When the amount of radiation detected _goes down_, it means the stuff is coming out _too thick_ and so the control unit _pinches the rollers up_ a bit to make it _thinner_ again.

4) If the reading _goes up_, it means it's _too thin_, so the control unit _opens the rollers out_ a bit.

5) The most important thing is the _choice of isotope_. First and foremost it must have a nice _long half-life_ (of several _years_ at least!), otherwise the strength would gradually _decline_ and the control unit would keep _pinching up_ the rollers trying to _compensate_.

6) Secondly, the source must be a _BETA source_ for _paper and cardboard_, or a _GAMMA source_ for _metal sheets_. This is because the stuff being made must _PARTLY_ block the radiation. If it _all_ goes through, (or _none_ of it does), then the reading _won't change_ at all as the thickness changes. Alpha particles are no use for this since they would _all be stopped_.

One other use of radioactivity is _sterilising food_ and _surgical instruments_ by exposing them to _gamma rays_.

Will any of that be in your Exam? — isotope so...

First _learn_ the three headings till you can write them down _from memory_. Then start _learning_ all the details that go with each one of them. As usual, the best way to check what you know is to do a _mini-essay_ for each section. Then check back and see what details you _missed_. Nicely.

Atomic Structure

See the Chemistry Book for a few more details on this.

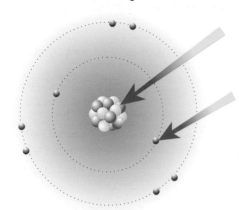

The _NUCLEUS_ contains _protons_ and _neutrons_.
Most of the _MASS_ of the atom is contained in the _nucleus_,
but it takes up virtually _no space_ — it's _tiny_.

The _ELECTRONS_ fly around the _outside_.
They're _negatively charged_ and really really _small_.
They occupy _a lot of space_ and this gives the atom its _overall size_,
even though it's mostly _empty space_.
The number of electrons is _equal to_ the number of protons.
This means that the whole atom has _no overall charge_.

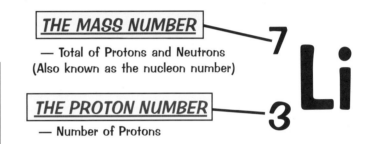

Make sure you _learn this table_:

PARTICLE	MASS	CHARGE
Proton	1	+1
Neutron	1	0
Electron	$\frac{1}{2000}$	- 1

THE MASS NUMBER

— Total of Protons and Neutrons
(Also known as the nucleon number)

THE PROTON NUMBER

— Number of Protons

$$^{7}_{3}\text{Li}$$

Isotopes _are_ Different Forms of The Same Element

1) All atoms of a _particular element_ have the _same number_ of protons.
2) _Isotopes_ are atoms with the _SAME_ number of protons but a _DIFFERENT_ number of neutrons.
3) Hence they have the _same proton number_, but _different mass number_.
4) _Carbon-12 and Carbon-14_ are good examples:
5) _Most elements_ have different isotopes but there's usually only one or two _stable_ ones.
6) Radioisotopes are _radioactive isotopes_, which means they _decay_ into other _elements_ and give out _radiation_. This is where all _radioactivity_ comes from — _unstable radioactive isotopes_ undergoing nuclear _decay_ and spitting out _high energy_ particles.

$$^{12}_{6}\text{C}$$ $$^{14}_{6}\text{C}$$

two extra neutrons

Rutherford's Scattering _and_ The Demise of the Plum Pudding

1) In 1804 _John Dalton_ said matter was made up of tiny _solid spheres_ which he called _atoms_.
2) Later they discovered _electrons_ could be _removed_ from atoms. They then saw atoms as _spheres_ of _positive charge_ with tiny negative electrons _stuck in them_ like plums in a _plum pudding_.
3) Then _Ernest Rutherford_ and his merry men tried firing _alpha particles_ at a _thin gold foil_. Most of them just went _straight through_, but the odd one came straight _back at them_, which was frankly a bit of a _shocker_ for Ernie and his pals.
4) Being pretty clued up guys though they realised this meant that _most_ of the mass of the atom was concentrated _at the centre_ in a _tiny nucleus_, with a _positive charge_.
5) This means that most of an atom is just made up of _empty space_, which is also _a bit of a shocker_ when you think about it.

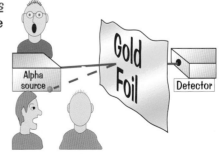

Alpha source

Gold Foil

Detector

Plum Pudding Theory — by 1911 they'd had their fill of it...

Yeah, that's right — atoms are mostly empty space. When you think about it, those electrons are amazing little jokers really. They have almost no mass, no size, and a tiny little –ve charge. In the end it's only their frantic whizzing about that makes atoms what they are. It's outrageous.

Nuclear Fission

Nuclear Fission — The Splitting Up of Uranium Atoms

Nuclear power stations and _nuclear submarines_ are both powered by _nuclear reactors_.
In a nuclear reactor, a controlled _chain reaction_ takes place in which uranium atoms _split up_ and _release energy_ in the form of _heat_. This heat is then simply used to _heat water_ to drive a _steam turbine_.
So nuclear reactors are really just _glorified steam engines_!

The Chain Reaction:

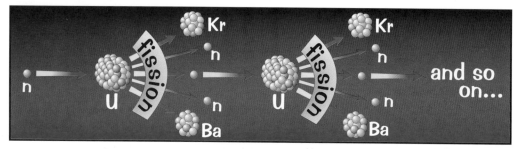

1) Each time a _uranium_ atom _splits up_, it spits out _two or three neutrons_, one of which hits _another_ uranium nucleus, causing it to _split_ also, and thus keeping the _chain reaction_ going.
2) When a uranium atom splits in two it will form _two new lighter elements_. These new nuclei are usually _radioactive_ because they have the "_wrong_" number of neutrons in them.
   This is the _big problem_ with nuclear power — it produces _huge_ amounts of _radioactive material_ which is very _difficult_ and _expensive_ to dispose of safely.
3) Each nucleus _splitting_ (called a _fission_) gives out _a lot of energy_ — a lot more energy than you get with a _chemical_ bond between two atoms. Make sure you remember that. _Nuclear processes_ release _much more energy_ than chemical processes do. That's why _nuclear bombs_ are _so much_ more powerful than ordinary bombs (which rely on _chemical_ reactions).

Decay Processes of α, β and γ Emission

1) Alpha Emission:

A typical _alpha-emission_:

$$^{226}_{88}Ra \rightarrow {}^{222}_{86}Rn + {}^{4}_{2}He$$

Unstable isotope → New isotope → Alpha particle

An α-_particle_ is simply a _helium nucleus_, mass 4 and charge of +2 made up of 2 protons and 2 neutrons.

2) Beta Emission:

A typical _beta-emission_:

$$^{14}_{6}C \rightarrow {}^{14}_{7}N + {}^{0}_{-1}e$$

Unstable isotope → New isotope → Beta particle

A β-_particle_ is simply an _electron_, with no mass and a charge of -1. _Every time_ a beta particle is emitted from the nucleus, a _neutron_ in the nucleus is _converted_ to a _proton_.

3) Gamma Emission:

A typical combined α– and γ–emission:
A γ-_ray_ is a _photon_ with no mass and no charge.

$$^{238}_{92}U \rightarrow {}^{234}_{90}Th + {}^{4}_{2}He + {}^{0}_{0}\gamma$$

Unstable isotope → New isotope → Gamma ray

After an _alpha or beta emission_ the nucleus sometimes has _extra energy to get rid of_. It does this by emitting a _gamma ray_. Gamma emission _never changes_ the _proton or mass numbers_ of the nucleus.

Alpha give the odd mistake — just don't beta lazy to learn it...

Learn all the details about chain reactions in nuclear fission with one easy mini-essay.
Also, more details about those three lovely types of radiation: alpha particles, beta particles and gamma rays. That's it so cover the page and jot down all the juicy details.

Half-life

The Radioactivity of a Sample Always Decreases Over Time

1) This is _pretty obvious_ when you think about it. Each time a _decay_ happens and an alpha, beta or gamma is given out, it means one more _radioactive_ nucleus has _disappeared_.

2) Obviously, as the _unstable nuclei_ all steadily disappear, the _activity_ as a whole will also _decrease_. So the _older_ a sample becomes, the _less_ radiation it will emit.

3) _How quickly_ the activity _drops off_ varies a lot from one radio-isotope to another. For _some_ it can take _just a few hours_ before nearly all the unstable nuclei have _decayed_, whilst others can last for _millions of years_.

4) The problem with trying to _measure_ this is that the activity _never reaches ZERO_, which is why we have to use the idea of _HALF-LIFE_ to measure how quickly the activity _drops off_.

5) Learn either of these _important definitions_ of _half-life_:

> HALF-LIFE is the TIME TAKEN for THE NUMBER OF PARENT atoms in a sample to HALVE

> HALF-LIFE is the TIME TAKEN for the ACTIVITY (or count rate) of the original substance to fall to HALF its ORIGINAL LEVEL

(The number of parent atoms is the number of atoms in the original radioactive source)

6) A _short half-life_ means the activity falls _quickly_, because _lots_ of the nuclei decay _quickly_.

7) A _long half-life_ means the activity falls _more slowly_ because _most_ of the nuclei don't decay for a _long time_ — they just sit there, basically _unstable_, but kind of _biding their time_.

Half-Life Calculations

Carbon-14 makes up a fairly constant 1/10 000 000 (One _ten-millionth_) of the carbon in the _air_, and the same proportion is also found in _living things_. However, when they _die_, the C-14 trapped _inside_ the wood or wool or whatever, gradually _decays_ with a _half-life_ of _5,600 years_. By simply measuring the _proportion_ of C-14 found in something you can easily calculate _how long ago_ the item was living material.

The basic idea of half-life is maybe a little confusing, but Exam calculations are _pretty straightforward_ so long as you do them slowly, STEP BY STEP. Like this one:

EXAMPLE: An axe handle was found to contain _1 part in 40 000 000_ C-14. Calculate the age of the axe.

ANSWER:
ORIGINAL proportion of C-14 was 1/10 000 000 → After ONE HALF LIFE... Proportion of C-14 is 1/20 000 000 → After TWO HALF-LIVES... Proportion of C-14 is 1/40 000 000

Hence the axe handle is _two C-14 half-lives_ old, i.e. 2 × 5,600 = _11,200 YEARS OLD_.

Uranium isotopes have a _very long_ half-life and decay via a _series_ of short-lived particles to produce _stable isotopes_ of lead. The _relative proportions_ of uranium and lead isotopes in a sample of _igneous_ rock can therefore be used to _date_ the rock, using the _known half-life_ of the Uranium (= 4.5 billion years). It's as simple as this:

INITIALLY:	After one half-life:	After two half-lives:	After three half-lives:
100% Uranium	50% Uranium	25% Uranium	12.5% Uranium
0% lead	50% lead	75% lead	87.5% lead

Ratio of Uranium to lead:
Initially	After _one half-life_	After _two half-lives_	After _three half-lives_
1:0	1:1	1:3	1:7

Similarly, the proportions of _potassium-40_ and its stable decay product _argon-40_ can be used to _date_ igneous rocks, so long as the _argon gas_ hasn't been able to _escape_. The _relative proportions_ are exactly the _same_ as for the uranium and lead example above.

Definition of Half-life — a freshly woken teenager...

People can get really confused by the idea of half-life. Remember — a radioactive sample will never completely decay away because the amount left just keeps halving. So the only way to measure how long it "lasts", is to time how long it takes to drop by half. That's all it is. Peasy

Revision Summary for Module Twelve

One thing's for sure — there are loads of fairly easy facts to learn about waves and radioactivity. Of course there are still some bits which need thinking about, but really, most of it is fairly easy stuff which just needs learning. Don't forget, this book contains all the important information which they've specifically mentioned in the syllabus, and this is precisely the stuff they're going to test you on in the Exams. You must practise these questions over and over again until they're easy.

1) Sketch a) a transverse wave, b) a longitudinal wave. Give a definition and four examples of each.
2) Define frequency, amplitude and wavelength for a wave and label the last two on your sketches above.
3) Sketch the patterns when plane ripples reflect at   a) a plane surface, b) a curved surface.
4) Sketch the reflection of curved ripples at a plane surface.
5) What is the law of reflection? Are sound and light reflected?
6) Find the speed of a wave with frequency 50kHz and wavelength 0.3cm.
7) What is refraction? What causes it? How does it affect wavelength and frequency?
8) Sketch a ray of light going through a rectangular glass block, showing the angles i and r. What if i=90°?
9) What is dispersion? Sketch the diagram which illustrates it with all the labels.
10) Sketch the three diagrams to illustrate Total Internal Reflection and the Critical Angle.
11) Sketch an application of total internal reflection which uses 45° prisms, and explain it.
12) Give details of the two main uses of optical fibres. How do optical fibres work?
13) What is diffraction? Sketch the diffraction of a) water waves b) sound waves c) light.
14) What aspect of EM waves determines their differing properties?
15) Sketch the EM spectrum with all its details. What happens when EM waves are absorbed?
16) Give full details of the uses of radio waves, microwaves and infrared.
17) Detail two uses of UV light, X-rays and gamma rays and say how harmful different dosages are.
18) What's the connection between amplitude and the energy carried by a wave?
19) What's the relationship between frequency and pitch for a sound wave?
20) Sketch CRO screens showing higher and lower pitch and quiet and loud sounds.
21) What is ultrasound? Give details of two applications of ultrasound.
22) What causes seismic waves? Sketch diagrams showing the paths of both types, and explain.
23) What do seismographs tell us about the structure of the Earth? Describe the Earth's inner structure.
24) Describe in detail the nature and properties of the three types of radiation: α, β, and γ.
25) How do the three types compare in penetrating power and ionising power? What blocks them?
26) Sketch a fairly accurate pie chart to show the six main sources of background radiation.
27) List three places where the level of background radiation is increased and explain why.
28) What damage does low doses cause to body cells?   What effects do higher doses have?
29) Which kind of sources are most dangerous a) inside the body   b) outside the body?
30) Describe in detail how radioactive isotopes are used in each of the following:
   a) tracers in medicine   b) tracers in industry   c) thickness control   d) treating cancer
31) Write down the number of electrons, protons and neutrons there are in an atom of $^{226}_{88}$Ra.
32) Explain what isotopes are. Give an example. Are most isotopes stable or unstable?
33) Describe Rutherford's Scattering Experiment with a diagram. What was concluded about the atom?
34) Draw a diagram to illustrate the fission of uranium and explain how the chain reaction works.
35) Describe the decay processes of: a) alpha particles b) beta particles c) gamma rays.
36) Give a proper definition of half-life. How long and how short can half-lives be?
37) A rock contains Uranium-238 atoms and stable lead atoms in the ratio 1:3.
   If the half-life of Uranium-238 is 4.5×10^9 years, how old is the rock?

Index

Index